Quick Guide

SHELVING & STORAGE

CREATIVE HOMEOWNER PRESS®

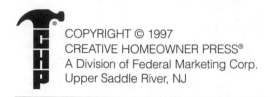

COPYRIGHT © 1997
CREATIVE HOMEOWNER PRESS®
A Division of Federal Marketing Corp.
Upper Saddle River, NJ

Editorial Director: David Schiff
Art Director: Annie Jeon

Author: Michael Presutti
Managing Editor: Timothy O. Bakke
Editorial Assistant: Georgette Blau
Copy Editor: Robin White Goode

Graphic Designer: Melisa DelSordo
Illustrator: Frank Rohrbach
Cover Design: Warren Ramezzana
Cover Illustrations: Craig Franklin

Electronic Prepress and Printed at:
Command Web Offset Co.

Current Printing (last digit)
10 9 8 7 6 5 4 3 2 1

Quick Guide: Shelving & Storage
Library of Congress Catalog Card Number: 97-60332
ISBN: 1-880029-91-X

CREATIVE HOMEOWNER PRESS®
A Division of Federal Marketing Corp.
24 Park Way
Upper Saddle River, NJ 07458

C O N T E N T S

SAFETY FIRST

Though all the designs and methods in this book have been tested for safety, it is not possible to overstate the importance of using the safest construction methods possible. What follows are reminders, some do's and don'ts of basic carpentry. They are not substitutes for your own common sense.

- *Always* use caution, care, and good judgment when following the procedures described in this book.

- *Always* be sure that the electrical setup is safe; be sure that no circuit is overloaded, and that all power tools and electrical outlets are properly grounded. Do not use power tools in wet locations.

- *Always* read container labels on paints, solvents, and other products; provide ventilation, and observe all other warnings.

- *Always* read the tool manufacturer's instructions for using a tool, especially the warnings.

- *Always* use holders or pushers to work pieces shorter than 3 inches on a table saw or jointer. Avoid working short pieces if you can.

- *Always* remove the key from any drill chuck (portable or press) before starting the drill.

- *Always* pay deliberate attention to how a tool works so that you can avoid being injured.

- *Always* know the limitations of your tools. Do not try to force them to do what they were not designed to do.

- *Always* make sure that any adjustment is locked before proceeding. For example, always check the rip fence on a table saw or the bevel adjustment on a portable saw before starting to work.

- *Always* clamp small pieces firmly to a bench or other work surfaces when sawing or drilling.

- *Always* wear the appropriate rubber or work gloves when handling chemicals, doing heavy construction, or sanding.

- *Always* wear a disposable face mask when working around odors, dust, or mist. Use a special filtering respirator when working with toxic substances.

- *Always* wear eye protection, especially when using power tools or striking metal on metal or concrete; a chip can fly off, for example, when chiseling concrete.

- *Always* be aware that there is seldom enough time for your body's reflexes to save you from injury from a power tool in a dangerous situation; everything happens too fast. Be *alert!*

- *Always* keep your hands away from the business ends of blades, cutters, and bits.

- *Always* hold a portable circular saw with both hands so that you will know where your hands are.

- *Always* use a drill with an auxiliary handle to control the torque when large size bits are used.

- *Always* check your local building codes when planning new construction. The codes are intended to protect public safety and should be observed to the letter.

- *Never* work with power tools when you are tired or under the influence of alcohol or drugs.

- *Never* cut very small pieces of wood or pipe. Whenever possible, cut small pieces off larger pieces.

- *Never* change a blade or a bit unless the power cord is unplugged. Do not depend on the switch being off; you might accidentally hit it.

- *Never* work in insufficient lighting.

- *Never* work while wearing loose clothing, hanging hair, open cuffs, or jewelry.

- *Never* work with dull tools. Have them sharpened, or learn how to sharpen them yourself.

- *Never* use a power tool on a workpiece that is not firmly supported or clamped.

- *Never* saw a workpiece that spans a large distance between horses without close support on either side of the kerf; the piece can bend, closing the kerf and jamming the blade, causing saw kickback.

- *Never* support a workpiece with your leg or other part of your body when sawing.

- *Never* carry sharp or pointed tools, such as utility knives, awls, or chisels, in your pocket. If you want to carry tools, use a special-purpose tool belt with leather pockets and holders.

MAXIMIZING SPACE

To maximize your storage space, keep the following considerations in mind: First, storage is efficient only when frequency of use is directly related to ease of accessibility. This means that the things you use most should be the easiest to get to. Second, before you store anything you must be mindful of the environmental conditions surrounding the stored items. Certain materials should not be stored in certain areas of the house unless they are properly protected. Third, always be aware of areas that have the potential to hold or hide your storables. Being creative about where you put things can solve many of your apparent storage problems.

Storage & Accessibility

Before you consider adding to or improving the storage capacity of your home, you must take an inventory of what you have on hand and get rid of what you don't need. Some of the items you're likely to find: old clothes that don't fit anymore or are out of style; tools, appliances, and toys that haven't been used in years; paperwork more than three or four years old. Almost anything you haven't used for a year or two is a candidate for simplifying your storage requirements. Once you've identified everything you can do without—and you may be surprised at how much that can be—hold a tag sale, send the items to a thrift shop, give them to friends, or simply throw them out. This process of taking stock of what

you have may seem a daunting task, but if you set aside a few hours to take care of one room or one closet at a time, you'll be surprised at how quickly you'll finish the job.

Now that you've identified your storage requirements, you need to categorize the items so you can store them in the most efficient way.

Frequent Use. When you need something every day or at least once a week, you'll want it close at hand. If you don't have enough room for these essentials, chances are you're storing other, unnecessary things in their place; you're simply not putting the important things first.

Look inside a kitchen cupboard or dresser drawer, and you may see things you haven't used in weeks or maybe months. This is an example of inefficient storage. Non-essential items like punch bowls, waffle irons,

rotisseries, pressure cookers, and the like are occupying the space that should be allotted to more frequently used items. Replacing these items will expand your storage capacity and make it much more efficient. It is perfectly acceptable to put these non-essential items up and away from day-to-day and week-to-week things. It is even feasible to tuck such items away in another area of the house altogether, like the basement, attic, or garage.

Seasonal Use. There are some items to which you need access only once a year or so. These items —important though they may be— can be put in a difficult-to-get-at area of the house. Here the lack of use justifies the extra degree of access difficulty: Think of holiday decorations, for instance. These items should be out of the way and literally not in sight.

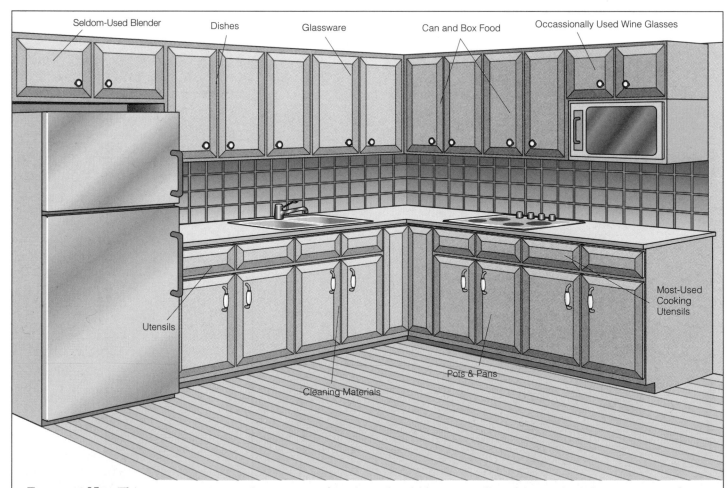

Frequent Use. Things you use every day or every few days should be put well within reach. Other items may be put in harder-to-reach or out-of-the-way places.

Environmental Conditions

Moisture

Of all destructive environmental conditions in and around the house, moisture is the worst. In fact, moisture is a contributing factor to almost every other destructive condition. You must be aware of those areas of the house that have humidity problems, and consider those problem areas in light of the items you plan to store there. The attic and basement are usually the most critical areas of humidity.

Basement. Humidity problems are most prevalent and consistent in the basement, where they can create a breeding ground for mold and mildew. All basements are at least partially underground, so they may be subject to condensation, or "sweating," in hot, humid weather and possibly to occasional ground-water infiltration.

To test for condensation and water seepage, tape pieces of aluminum foil to various places on the wall and floor. Seal the edges tightly and leave the test patches in place for several days. If moisture droplets appear beneath the foil, moisture is migrating through the masonry and nothing short of a major water-proofing project will improve the condition. Don't use the basement for storage until the problem is corrected. If moisture droplets appear on top of the foil, the problem is condensation from basement humidity. You can solve a humidity problem in a few ways, but it's easiest simply to use a dehumidifier to dry out the air.

Paper products, fabrics, and other organic materials are affected by high humidity levels. If you store items like these in the basement, seal them in plastic containers and store them high off the floor.

When at all possible, avoid putting organic items like these in the basement unless you run a dehumidifier or live in an extremely dry climate. If you must store clothes, linens, fabrics, and the like in plastic, place cedar chips in along with them.

For inorganic materials like metal, the concern is rust. If conditions are severe, there is little you can do to prevent metal from rusting. Keep these kinds of things away from humid storage areas.

Attic. The sensitivity of various materials to humidity fluctuations is a concern in the attic. Every day, the attic's relative humidity changes in direct proportion to the relative humidity outside. On a rainy day, the relative humidity in your attic will likely be high. In fair weather, the relative humidity in the attic will be low.

Here, too, organic material may be at risk. Humidity fluctuations can speed the decay of certain items. Clothing, linens, fabrics, and paper products stored in the attic are best stored in wooden trunks or chests. The wooden container surrounding the items creates a

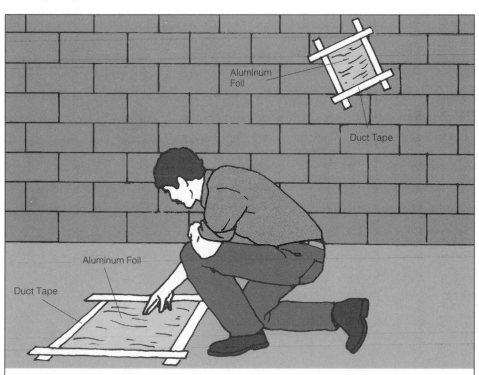

Basement. Tape aluminum foil to the floor and wall. Moisture droplets on top indicate humidity problems; moisture underneath points to seepage problems.

more stable environment and, in effect, reduces the fluctuation of humidity inside the container over time. Using cedar chests or cedar-lined trunks is an ideal way to guard against this problem.

Temperature

The attic and garage have identical temperature fluctuations and freeze-thaw cycles. In most parts of the country, temperatures fall below freezing in the attic and garage during at least part of the winter, and summertime temperatures can rise above 100 degrees.

Though not a major concern for most stored organic materials, freeze-thaw cycles can damage products made of combinations of dissimilar mater-ials like wood, glass, and steel. Because dissimilar materials expand and contract at different rates, freezing and thawing tend to undermine the structure of the product. In time, the piece will lose its structure and literally fall apart.

Insects and Pests

Wood products and cardboard boxes containing books, clothing, linens, furs, and the like can be fertile ground for various insects and pests when stored in the attic, basement, or garage. In most cases, termites and rodents like mice are the main concerns, and you'll find that guarding against them, in effect, guards against almost every other insect and pest.

Termites. There are approximately 55 termite species in the United States. They can be grouped into two basic groups; subterranean and non-subterranean termites. Subterranean termites live in the ground and need moisture, while non-subterranean termites inhabit wooden structures like fallen trees and wooden objects close to the ground. Subterranean termites account for most of the damage to residential homes in the East and Northeast, while non-subterranean, or "dry wood," termites are generally found in the Southand West.

Subterranean termites live in colonies. At certain times of the year winged males and females swarm from the colony, fly a short distance (4 to 10 feet), shed their wings, and if possible, start new colonies. Sub-terranean termites do not establish themselves in buildings by being carried there in lumber but enter from ground nests after the building has been constructed.

Subterranean termites build their tun-nels in dirt and nearby buried wood-en obstructions. They start there and tunnel to get at more wood, which they need for nutri-tion. Termites also need ample moisture. Damp, dark locations with scattered construction de-bris are perfect locations for new subterranean termite colonies.

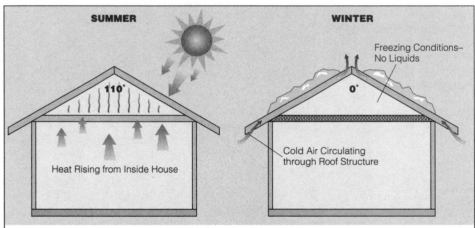

Temperature. Attic temperatures can fluctuate by more than 100 degrees F between winter and summer months.

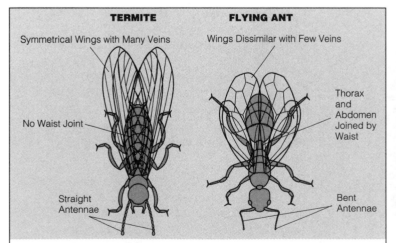

Termites. Ants and termites differ significantly in the shapes of their bodies and wings.

Signs of Termite Infestation. Poke the framing in the header- and rim-joist areas to look for soft wood indicating insect damage.

Signs of Termite Infestation.

Termites leave telltale calling cards when they invade your house. Here's what to look for:

■ Tubular "vines" made of earth that termites use as pathways along inedible surfaces like foundations or concrete slabs to get at the edible wood above.

■ Swarming of winged adults early in the spring or fall. Don't mistake termites for flying ants, however, which resemble winged termites but are harmless. Try to capture an individual and distinguish it as either a termite or a flying ant.

■ Piles of fecal pellets outside or near wood. These piles will resemble sawdust.

■ The appearance of discarded termite wings on the window sills or near the sill of the basement and or attic.

■ Soft or hollowed wood members. Since termites destroy the center of wooden members, wood sills and joists will appear normal. Poking the wood with a pocket knife or ice pick will provide you with evidence of their existence.

Mice and Other Rodents.

If not the most common, mice are the most stereotypical household invaders. Mice are relentless in their quest for warm nesting grounds, and their favorite spots seem to be garages, sheds, and—when they can manage it—homes. You'd be amazed at the tight spots they can crawl through. A determined mouse can squeeze through a crack less than ½ inch wide. Mice sometimes may take up residence in the basement or attic and never make it to the house proper. But even in these cases, they can cause havoc by nesting in stored clothing or fabric and ruining it. Besides, just having mice in the vicinity is enough to send shills up the spines of some homeowners.

If you have mice, you'll know it in short order. You'll be able to hear them scratching in walls, floors, and ceilings, especially at night. You may see droppings, especially in drawers and on countertops and shelves. And you may see holes chewed through cardboard boxes or edges gnawed off pieces of wood framing in their way.

Ways to Prevent Infestation.

You can take precautions to avoid problems with termites, rodents, and other pests in the first place.

■ Don't leave wood scraps lying around the house. Remember too that paper is wood and that buried paper and cardboard are also attractive to termites.

■ Plants and shrubbery against the house encourage ideal moist conditions for insects and allow them access to the house. Flower planters are common termite targets because you supply them with two essentials: wood and water.

■ Pipes, utilities, exterior sill cocks, and other protrusions through the basement wall can have cracks that allow insects and mice to enter. Caulk all openings with a silicone or mastic caulking.

■ Wooden trellises, stakes, fences, or other ornaments attached to the house can provide access for termites and carpenter ants. Remove such structures and replace them with a similar one made of inedible, or non-wood, materials.

■ Wooden porch steps are literally stairways for termites. These steps should always be made of pressure-treated wood or masonry. Wood siding also poses this threat. Make sure the bottom of the wall's siding is at least 6 inches from the ground. In places where termite infestations are common, install a termite shield—a bent strip of aluminum that the subterranean termites have difficulty traveling over.

■ Crawl spaces with soil under them are pathways for termites and other pests. Cover the crawl-space floor with a sheet of polyethylene. Lap all joints by at least 12 inches and make sure the sheet is sealed tightly around the perimeter where the plastic meets the concrete.

■ Wooden posts buried in the ground are likely targets for termites. Even those with concrete bases are commonly vulnerable from below. Always use treated posts and/or masonry to support wooden structures above.

■ Cracked slabs and foundations are the most common entryway for subterranean insects and mice. Fill and/or repair all cracks wider than about ⅜ inch.

Note: For eradicating or controlling insects and other pests, contact a pest-control professional in your area. They are licensed to handle the chemicals needed to do the job.

Storage & Organization

Getting Started

The projects and ideas in this book will help you with your storage needs throughout the house; they are presented in a practical room-by-room format. Of course, ideas can often be applied to a number of rooms or situations, and most projects can be adjusted to your particular storage needs. In many cases actual project sizes have been left to your discretion, but typical standards have been indicated when necessary.

With flexibility of design in mind, the size relationships between project components have been indicated. For example, "the shelf will be 1½ inches less than the top section" denotes a relationship between the "shelf" and the "top section," regardless of the actual project or component size. In this way you can be creative and alter the project to suit your specific needs. Standards and preferred sizes have also been illustrated.

Putting Dead Spaces to Work

Throughout this book, you'll see suggestions that will help you better use the space you have. At the cornerstone of good storage is creativity. If you look around your house, you'll probably find lots of "dead," or wasted, spaces. You'll discover how to use these spaces to store things in closets, under staircases, in corners, and under furniture. The trick is to be creative.

Closets. If you examine your closets, you'll probably also find lots of dead space there owing to an inefficient use of the entire closet area. Manufactured coated-wire and laminated-particleboard storage systems can help greatly in using a closet efficiently. If you'd rather make closet storage systems yourself out of plywood, you'll find projects to help you along those lines as well (pages 43 to 44).

Under Stairs. The area under a staircase is fertile ground for harvesting extra storage space around the house. This is especially true in the basement, where the under-stairs area is more apt to be open to the surrounding space. The best way to make use of the space under staircases is to close it off and organize it with shelving or built-in drawers (page 76). The drawers can be made of wood, or they can be coated-wire frame types.

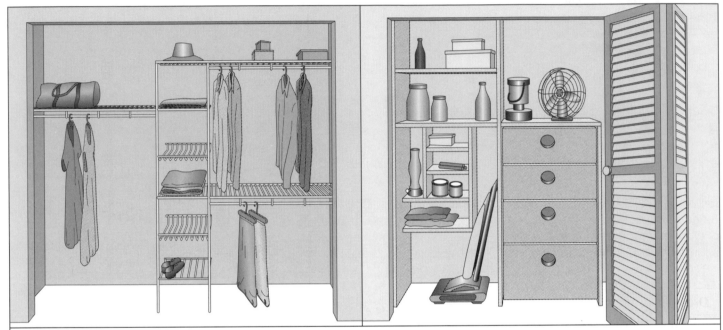

Closets. Coated-wire (left) and laminated-particleboard (right) organizers can make storage easier and your closets more useful.

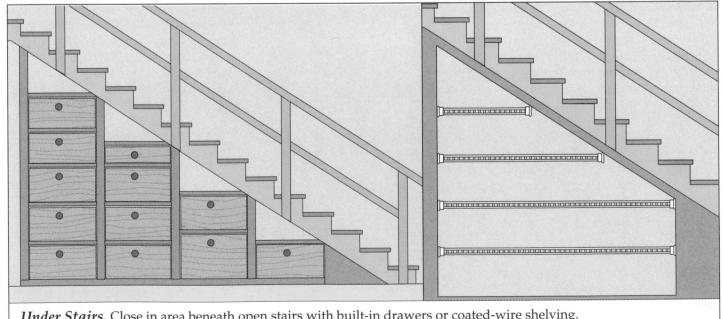

Under Stairs. Close in area beneath open stairs with built-in drawers or coated-wire shelving.

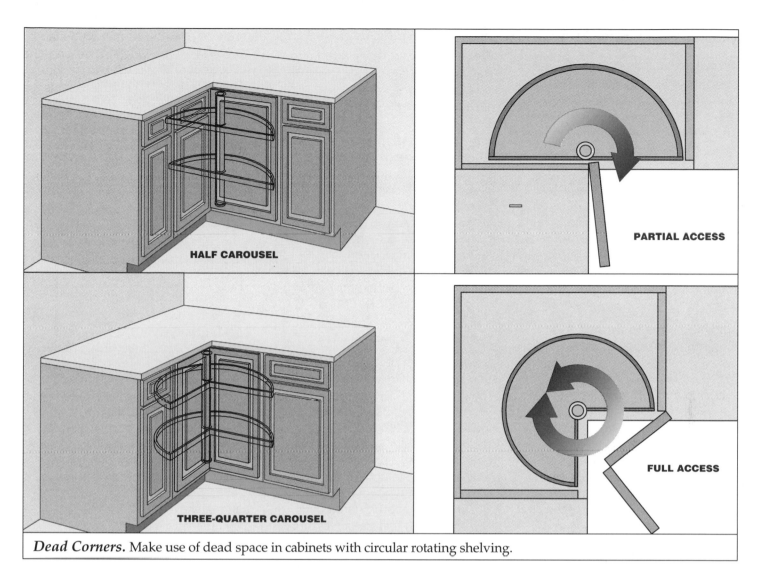

HALF CAROUSEL

PARTIAL ACCESS

THREE-QUARTER CAROUSEL

FULL ACCESS

Dead Corners. Make use of dead space in cabinets with circular rotating shelving.

Dead Corners. There are many areas of the house where you can put ordinarily wasted corner space to work. Use a Lazy Susan in a kitchen corner cabinet so things don't get lost in its dark recesses, or you could set up a recycling center (page 35). Build a window seat under a window near the corner of a room or between two close walls—in a dormer, for example (page 53). Hang netting across the corner over a child's bed to hold stuffed animals and lightweight toys (page 53).

Under Furniture. Just about every parent knows about cleaning under children's beds. Toys, games, clothes, and the like seem to accumulate there almost by themselves. You can organize this otherwise wasted, often cluttered space by using pull-out under-bed drawers (page 48).

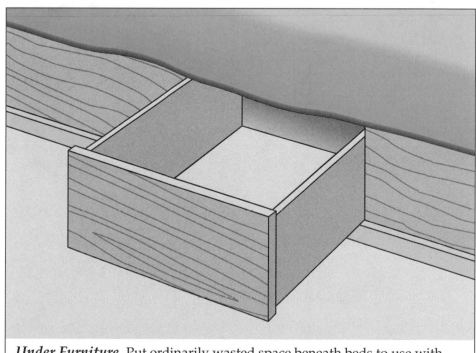

Under Furniture. Put ordinarily wasted space beneath beds to use with rolling drawers.

Efficient Work Habits. Often the hardest part of a home improvement project is maintaining enthusiasm throughout the job. It's easy to get discouraged or frustrated if things don't go according to plan. Here are some hints that will help you through these times.

Being Prepared. Plan out your project in detail and make sure all your materials and tools are on the job. Being prepared will allow you to work without any interruptions. It also saves precious time. Running around town trying to buy odds and ends on a Saturday morning can destroy the whole day.

Allowing Time to Complete a Project. Allow ample time to collect your thoughts, set your plan of action, and perform your task cautiously. Hurrying through a job can lead to sloppiness and sometimes accidents. Remember—you're not paying yourself by the hour. Sometimes the only difference between professionals' work and that of non-professionals is that professionals can do it in a fraction of the time because they're so experienced. So if you want professional results, don't rush your work.

Following Safety Precautions. Pay close attention to the safety precautions at the beginning of this book. Wear eye protection such as safety goggles or plastic glasses whenever you work with tools or chemicals. It's a good idea to purchase an extra pair for those times when a neighbor volunteers to lend a hand, or when you misplace your own pair. Make sure the eye protection conforms to requirements set by the American National Standards Institute (ANSI) or Canadian Standards Association (CSA). Products that meet these requirements will indicate that fact with a stamp.

Since airborne particles such as sawdust and the like are an inevitable by-product of almost any project, it's a good idea to wear a dust mask, especially when using power tools like circular saws, sanders, and drills. Two types of masks are available: disposable dust masks and cartridge-type respirators. A dust mask is good for protecting you from most fine particles. Respirators generally offer superior protection, but they also have certain disadvantages. With a respirator, breathing is more labored and it can get warm inside the mask. Whichever you purchase, be sure that it has been stamped by the National Institute for Occupational Safety & Health/Mine Safety and Health Administration (NIOSH/MSHA) and is approved for your specific operation. If you can taste or smell the contaminate, or if the mask starts to interfere with normal breathing, it's time for a replacement.

The U.S. Occupational Safety and Health Administration (OSHA) recommends that hearing protection be worn whenever the noise level exceeds 85 decibels (dB) for an 8-hour workday. Considering that a circular saw emits 110 dB, even shorter exposure times can eventually lead to hearing loss. Insert and muff-type protectors are available; make sure that the model you choose has a noise reduction rating (NRR) of at least 20 dB. Lastly, wear safety gloves with leather palms when you use materials that can irritate or puncture your skin.

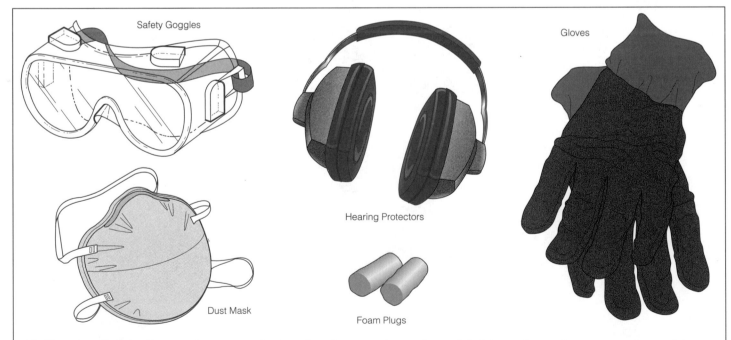

Following Safety Precautions. Avoid injury by always using safe work habits and wearing appropriate safety equipment when necessary.

TOOLS, MATERIALS & TECHNIQUES

This chapter describes the tools and materials you'll need to complete the projects in this book, ranging from simple hand tools to power tools and accessories. You'll also find information on joinery techniques and materials for assembling custom-made storage systems.

Tools for Manufactured Storage Systems

Assembling storage-unit kits, coated-wire closet organizers, and adjustable shelving systems usually entails a limited range of skills: measuring, drilling holes, driving screws, and attaching bolts. You'll need an assortment of hand-held tools to complete these tasks.

Measuring Tape. Measuring tapes commonly come in lengths ranging from 6 to 50 feet. A 16-footer will accommodate any project in this book.

Level. A level may be made of wood, metal, or plastic. You'll use a level to determine whether a shelving or storage-unit member is horizontal (level) or vertical (plumb). New electronic digital levels can check other angles as well.

Stud Finder. To make sure you'll screw or nail into studs on a finished wall, use a magnetic or electronic stud finder.

Electric Drill. Manufactured shelving systems usually come packaged with wall fasteners, but you'll have to drill holes to accommodate them. Look for a variable-speed, reversible ⅜-inch drill for both drilling and driving screws. Cordless drills may be more expensive, but they're the most convenient to work with because they can be used anywhere without an extension cord.

Invest in a set of twist-drill bits with sizes from ¹⁄₁₆ to ¼ inch; you can always buy larger sizes as you need them. You'll also want screwdriver bits.

Screwdrivers. Although you may use a variable-speed drill for driving screws quickly, there will be times when you'll need an old-fashioned screwdriver. It may rank as one of the simplest tools found in any toolbox, but a good set of screwdrivers is essential for the do-it-yourselfer. Flat-bladed and Phillips screwdrivers are the two most common.

Pliers and Wrenches. Adjustable pliers may be used to tighten or loosen fittings or to hold a nut as you tighten a screw or bolt during assembly. Wrenches do an even better job of tightening or loosening nuts and bolts. An adjustable wrench has a movable jaw and a fixed jaw, with a worm-screw adjustment that lets you set the size of the opening between the jaws. Open-end and box wrenches provide a stronger grip than an adjustable wrench does and can be purchased in sets containing a variety of sizes. Socket wrenches, which ratchet for easy turning of nuts and bolts, are the most convenient wrenches to use in most cases.

Hammer. A 16- or 20-ounce claw hammer is the first choice for driving and removing nails and brads. It's also good for striking stubborn bolts, nail sets, and punches, and for nudging together pieces of an assembly that are a tight fit.

Tools for Custom-Built Systems

Custom-building storage units and shelving requires some woodworking skill and a bigger toolbox. Besides basic carpentry tools, you'll need a small selection of power tools and specialty tools and materials.

Squares

The four most common squares in the home workshop are the angle square, combination square, framing square, and try square. They're used for measuring, marking, and checking the inside and outside squareness of right angles. Other useful squares include the sliding bevel and T-square.

Angle Square. Use the angle, or speed, square as a depth gauge or protractor, or for scribing lines at 45 and 90 degrees. It also doubles as a circular saw guide for crosscutting.

Combination Square. The combination square is one of the most useful

Tools for Manufactured Storage Systems

Stud Finder

Wrench

Drill

Hammer

Socket Wrench

Adjustable Wrench

Pliers

Screwdrivers

Measuring Tape

Level

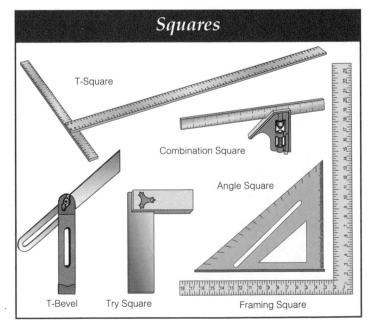

Squares

T-Square

Combination Square

Angle Square

T-Bevel

Try Square

Framing Square

tools in any woodworker's shop. You can use it horizontally to check for level, vertically to check for plumb, or diagonally as a miter square. It serves as an inside try square, outside try square, depth gauge, marking gauge, and straightedge.

Framing Square. This square is available in a few sizes. The larger version, which has a 24-inch-long blade and 16-inch-long tongue, is the tool of choice for framing work. You may find one of the smaller models, measuring 8 x 6 or 12 x 8 inches, more convenient for smaller projects.

Sliding Bevel. Also known as the T-bevel, sliding T-bevel, or bevel square, this simple tool is commonly used for transferring and duplicating angles other than 90-degrees.

T-square. Another useful square is the 48-inch T-square, sometimes called a drywall square. It's ideal for working with gypsum wallboard, paneling, plywood, hardboard, and other sheet stock.

Try Square. Use a try square to test, or try, the squareness of right angles, to scribe lines, and to calibrate tools.

Hammers, Chisels & Planes

Every woodworker should be armed with at least three basic hammers: a claw hammer, a tack hammer, and a mallet. Each has a specific purpose. You'll use chisels and planes for precise wood removal.

Claw Hammer. For cabinet and other fine work, you're best off using a small 12-ounce hammer, but you can get away with using a 16-ounce hammer.

Tack Hammer. When you need to drive tacks or brads that are just too tiny to grip, you'll appreciate the magnetic head on your tack hammer.

Mallet. Use a wooden mallet or soft-faced hammer whenever a metal hammer might damage a surface.

Wood Chisels. Designed for removing wood in chips, chunks, and shavings, wood chisels can be driven with a mallet or manipulated by hand for precise paring.

Planes. Although you could build every project in this book without ever having to reach for one, few tools can remove paper-thin shavings of wood or smooth a rough board as quickly or precisely as an old-fashioned hand plane.

Clamps

No shop ever has enough clamps, yet these essential tools are most often overlooked by beginning do-it-yourselfers. Clamps are designed for such jobs as edge-gluing boards (see page 61) and attaching trim to plywood edges. It won't take long for you to discover how valuable they can be throughout your shop. Use clamps to secure workpieces for sawing, routing, drilling, or sanding. A good basic starter set consists of a pair or two of 4-inch C-clamps and at least one pair of pipe clamps.

Bar Clamps. Bar clamps provide greater reach than most other clamps and are ideal for drawing frame members and cabinet panels together. They range in size from about 12 to 96 inches.

Corner Clamps. These clamps are designed to hold two pieces of material together at a right angle for gluing, nailing, or screwing.

Pipe Clamps. Available from home centers, hardware stores, and mail-order sources, pipe clamps offer a less expensive alternative to bar types for big clamping tasks. These clamps consist of cast-iron fixtures that you thread onto lengths of separately purchased black-iron pipe.

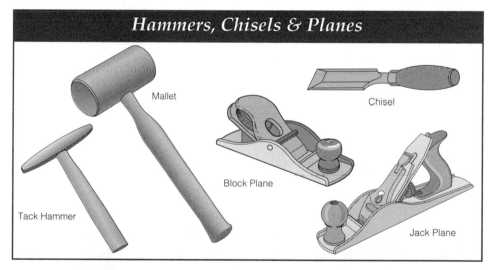

Hammers, Chisels & Planes

Mallet

Chisel

Block Plane

Tack Hammer

Jack Plane

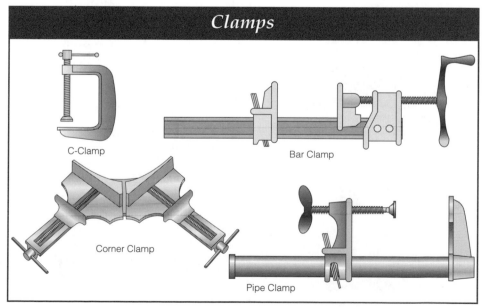

Clamps

C-Clamp

Bar Clamp

Corner Clamp

Pipe Clamp

Other Helpful Hand Tools

In addition to the hand tools listed above, you'll need some other tools to help with the projects.

Saws. One of the most important hand-tool combinations in any woodworker's shop is the miter box and backsaw. Backsaws come with blades ranging from 12 to 30 inches long.

You'll need a handsaw for some cuts you can't make with power saws and a hacksaw for cutting metal. You may find you need a coping saw for some decorative curves, and you might want to buy a flush-cutting saw for special chores such as flush-cutting wood plugs.

Utility Knife. Not only is a utility knife useful for the projects listed in this book, but it's a great tool to have for other tasks.

Nail Sets and Punches. A nail set is used to drive nails below the work surface without causing dents, so the holes can be easily filled. A set rests on top of a nail or brad, enabling you to sink the nail without damaging the surrounding wood.

A center punch looks like a nail set, except that its sharp, conical point tends to stick into wood. You'll need one for locating and punching starter holes for twist-drill bits to keep them from "walking" off their mark during the initial drilling.

Power Tools

To do some of the projects in this book, power tools will come in handy: a saber saw and/or circular saw, router, and electric sander. You can get by without any stationary power tools, but a table saw can save a lot of time when you need to cut sheet stock, mill grooves or rabbets, or tackle a variety of other sawing chores.

Portable Power Saws

Saber Saw. Use a saber saw with a saw guide to cut straight lines or freehand to make pocket cuts, circular cuts, and other cuts of unusual shape. A saber saw is excellent for cutting and trimming panel stock, back-cutting large moldings, and making cutouts in countertops.

Circular Saw. This workhorse is as indispensable in the home workshop as it is on a commercial construction site. The standard circular saw uses a 7¼-inch blade that can crosscut or rip stock up to 2½ inches thick, which means the saw will easily handle nominal 1- and 2-inch lumber and all sheet stock.

Router, Bits & Accessories

The router ranks just behind drills and saws in popularity among woodworkers. This versatile tool deserves its place in the workshop because of its capacity to perform a tremendous variety of tasks such as making rabbets, dadoes, and grooves; routing decorative edges in wood; making moldings; and cutting plastic laminates.

All routers are basically a motor mounted on a base. The wide range in price largely reflects differences in power: ⅓- to ½-horsepower (hp) models are considered light-duty, while heavy-duty models are powered with 2- to 3-hp motors. If you're buying a single router for general purposes, get one rated at about 1½ horsepower.

Basic Bits. Outfit your router with a set of basic bits including straight, roundover, rabbeting, cove, and chamfering bits. If you plan to laminate your countertops, you'll also need a flush-trimming bit.

Router Table. You can buy or build a router table. This accessory lets your router function like a small shaper. A table is ideal for many applications, when it's easier or safer to bring the material to the tool, instead of vice versa.

Sanders

No chore is as tedious as hand sanding. A general-duty electric sander will save untold amounts of time and will help produce a more uniform finish.

Pad Sander. Also known as finishing sanders, pad sanders are available in three popular sizes to accommodate sheets of sandpaper in ¼-, ⅓-, or ½-sheet sizes.

Random-Orbit Disc Sander. This sander is popular with woodworkers because it removes wood faster than

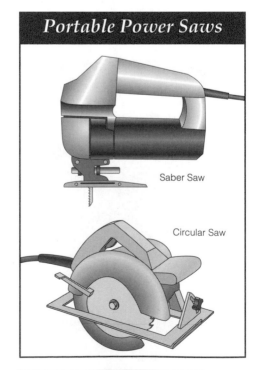

Portable Power Saws

Saber Saw

Circular Saw

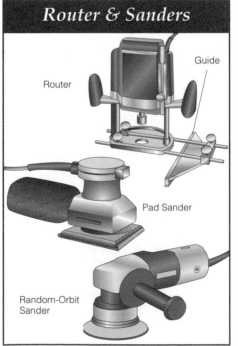

Router & Sanders

Router

Guide

Pad Sander

Random-Orbit Sander

a pad sander, while its random orbit eliminates the swirls you may get with a pad sander.

Table Saw, Blades, Accessories

The most valuable, versatile tool for any serious home workshop is the table saw. It's available in a variety of sizes and prices, ranging from inexpensive 8-inch bench-top models for just over $100 to the 12-inch industrial powerhouses that cost more than $2,000. The 10-inch saw is most popular among woodworkers. Most bench-top and some free-standing models are "motorized," meaning the saw arbor is attached directly to the motor. Better saws are belt-driven, making them work smoother, stronger, and quieter than motorized saws.

Blades. Steel blades cost between $10 and $20; carbide-tipped blades go from $10 to more than $200. The usual rule applies: Buy the best you can afford. For general purposes, buy a 40- or 50-tooth combination blade. For making clean, splinter-free cuts in plywood and other materials, buy an 80-tooth blade designed for such purposes.

Dado Cutters. A table saw equipped with a dado cutter can make short work of cutting dadoes, grooves, and rabbets. Depending on the style and manufacturer of the cutter, most are capable of cutting widths ranging from ¼ to ¹³⁄₁₆ inch.

One type of dado cutter blade is called a wobbler or wobble saw. When this single-blade cutter is installed in the table saw, its offset blade oscillates, or wobbles, creating a kerf that's wider than the usual ⅛ inch. A problem with this style cutter is that it tends to dish out the bottoms of the grooves.

Another type of cutter is called a stacked dado cutter set or simply a dado set. This type consists of two cutters that resemble combination blades and a set of chippers and shims. The width of the cut is determined by installing different shims and chippers between the blades. Stacked cutters will not dish out the bottoms of dadoes and are less likely than a wobbler to splinter the wood. Stacked cutters are more expensive.

Materials

With a little plywood, particleboard, and/or various kinds of moldings, you'll be able to build most of the custom storage units presented in this book!

Plywood

Plywood is made from thin veneers of wood glued together in a sand-wich. Each veneer is oriented perpendicular to the next, which makes plywood stronger and more resistant to warping than solid wood. Plywood is available with either softwood or hardwood surface veneers and is sold in 4x8-foot sheets; many home centers also stock half and quarter sheets. Common thicknesses range from ⅛ to ¾ inch.

Particleboard

Particleboard is a term used to describe several different types of sheet material made from ground-up bits of wood and adhesive. Particle-board isn't much to look at, but because it's stable and considerably cheaper than plywood, it's typically used as an underlayment for plastic laminates and wood veneers.

Some of the benefits of working with particleboard are that it doesn't warp, shrink, or swell with changes in humidity. On the downside, particleboard is heavy and tends to sag under a load more than plywood or solid wood. Particleboard chips easily and doesn't hold fasteners well; it's best to use special particleboard fasteners instead of wood screws. Always use carbide-tipped blades when cutting particleboard because it will dull a steel blade in a few passes.

Particleboard, like plywood, is available in 4x8-foot sheets. It also comes in a variety of board and panel widths up to 16 inches that can be used for shelving. Thicknesses range from ¼ to ¾ inch.

Hardboard

Hardboard is made from wood fibers bonded with pressure and heat to form a thin, durable panel. It's normally used where it can't be seen, such as for drawer bottoms and rear panels for cabinets. Like particleboard, hardboard will dull your saw blades quickly, so cut it with a carbide-tipped blade.

Perforated Hardboard. Also known as pegboard or perf-board, perfo-rated hardboard is often used as wall

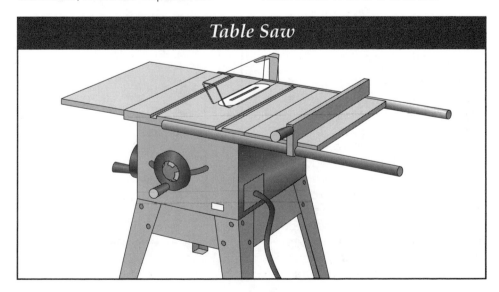

Table Saw

material in workshops and garages where it serves as a place to hang tools and other items. It also serves the same purpose in some specialized closets and cabinets.

Tempered Hardboard. Both plain and perforated hardboard are available as tempered products, which are impregnated with resin to make them stronger and more resistant to moisture. Hardboard is highly susceptible to humidity fluctuations, which can cause it to warp and buckle. So always buy tempered hardboard, which costs only a little more than the standard product.

Fasteners & Hardware

Every home center and hardware store seems to have an endless variety of mechanical fasteners and an overwhelming assortment of hardware for every imaginable purpose. The basic building blocks for all the projects in this book are nails or screws and glue. Although screws are considerably stronger than nails, glue is the most important fastener in any wood joint. A good glue joint can be stronger than the wood itself.

Nails

Common Types of Nails. The five main types of nails are box nails, brads, casing nails, common nails, and finishing nails. Use box and common nails for rough work such as utility shelving and storage units; use finishing and casing nails for cabinetry and trim, respectively. Casing nails have a slightly larger diameter than finishing nails and a more tapered head. Both finishing and casing nails come with either dimpled or smooth heads; the dimpled heads are easier to countersink with a nail set. Brads resemble finishing nails, except they are much smaller. Brads are used for attach-ing small moldings and other thin materials.

Screws

Screws come in a great variety of diameter and length combinations. They're identified by the thickness or gauge of their shafts and by their lengths, followed by head type. A flathead screw with a 10-gauge thickness and length of 3½ inches would be labeled as #10 x 3½-inch flathead. The two kinds of screws you'll need for the projects in this book are wood screws and drywall screws.

Wood and Drywall Screws. Wood screws are tapered so the threads bite into the wood, which makes a stronger bond than you get using nails. Screws take longer to install, however, because most installations, especially in hardwood, require a pilot hole for each screw. Also, most screw holes must be countersunk or counterbored to drop the screwhead below the surface of the wood.

One kind of screw that's gained favor among carpenters and cabinetmakers is the drywall screw, also known as the all-purpose, or buglehead, screw. These screws don't require a pilot hole in softwoods; their aggressive threads are designed to drive fast and hold tight. In addition, the screws are self-countersinking in most softwoods. The screw's Phillips head is extra deep to prevent stripping and make driving easy with power drivers.

Specialty Fasteners

It's best to attach shelving and other built-ins to wall studs with conventional nails and screws. But many projects, especially closet organizers, can't be installed that way. For example, hollow plaster or drywall and solid masonry walls pose special problems that must be solved with specialty fasteners such as toggle bolts, hollow-wall anchors, and expansion shields.

Hollow-Wall Fasteners. Toggle bolts and other hollow-wall anchors are designed for use in plaster or drywall walls. A toggle bolt has spring-loaded wings that open against the inside of the wall as the bolt is tightened. It's probably the most secure hollow-wall fastener. Instead of wings, a hollow-wall expansion anchor has a sleeve that expands against the inside of the wall. Drivable wall anchors, plastic-wing anchors, and wallboard twist anchors grip the wall material and accept screws for holding moderate weight. Most closet-organizing systems come with their own variation of hollow-wall anchor, usually a plastic expansion anchor or a variation of the plastic-wing anchor.

Solid-Wall Fasteners. Fasteners for use in brick or concrete walls usually take the form of bolts that fit

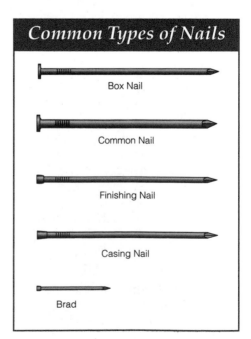

Common Types of Nails

- Box Nail
- Common Nail
- Finishing Nail
- Casing Nail
- Brad

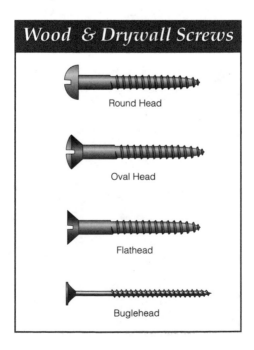

Wood & Drywall Screws

- Round Head
- Oval Head
- Flathead
- Buglehead

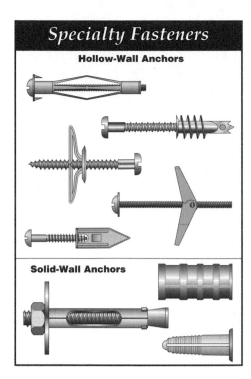
into expansion shields or anchors of some kind, or plastic anchors used with wood screws. To use masonry anchors, drill holes the same diameter as the anchors into the wall. Gently tap the anchors into the holes with a hammer. Install anchor bolts or screws, which will cause the anchors to expand as the screws are tightened.

Adhesives

You'll need only a couple types of adhesive for just about any custom-built storage project you'll tackle from this book.

Carpenter's Wood Glue. Aliphatic resin glue, commonly called carpenter's glue or yellow glue, is the adhesive of choice for bonding wood to wood. This kind of glue sets quickly and can be cleaned up with water, and it's sandable.

Contact Cement. This rubber-based liquid glue bonds on contact. Use to join plastic laminate or other veneers to a solid-wood, plywood, or particleboard underlayment. Apply contact cement to both surfaces, and allow it to dry for approximately 15 minutes before joining the parts. The parts will stick together immediately upon contact.

Techniques

The joinery and other techniques explained here include those that are widely applicable to the projects in this book. Some techniques appear in this chapter so that they needn't be repeated with each project. Wherever necessary, these techniques have been conveniently cross-referenced.

Cutting & Trimming Plywood

One way to break panels down to manageable size is to make free-hand cuts with a portable circular saw, running the saw along a layout line. Freehand cuts are not accurate enough for most cabinet work, however. So begin by using a portable circular saw to rip panels about ¼ inch oversize. Then rip them to final width on the table saw, guiding the factory edges against the rip fence.

Even after panels are ripped to width, many are too long and wide to crosscut to length on the table saw. Instead, make your crosscuts with the portable circular saw, guiding the saw against a straightedge, or better yet, make a straight-cutting jig.

Making a Straight-Cutting Jig

Guiding a circular saw along a simple straightedge is tricky because the straightedge must be offset from the cut line by a distance that's exactly equal to the distance between the edge of the saw base and the blade. The straight-cutting jig is custom-cut to your saw and blade so you can set the edge of the jig right on the cut line.

1 Assembling the Jig. The jig is simply a straight-edged board that's glued to a hardboard base. For your straightedge, use any length of plywood or solid lumber that has two straight edges and is at least 2 inches wide. Fasten the straightedge to a length of ⅛-inch-thick tempered hardboard with glue and screws, allowing about 8 inches of hardboard on both sides. Screw through the hardboard into the straightedge, and countersink the screws slightly.

2 Trimming the Jig. Once the glue has dried, trim off one side of the base. To do this, square the blade to the base of the saw, adjust the depth of cut to ¼ inch, and place the jig on a scrap of plywood. When you make the cut, run the edge of the circular saw's base against the straightedge. This will create a straight base edge that shows the saw's exact cutting line.

To use the jig, clamp it onto the workpiece and align the edge of the base along the cutting line. Place the clamps along the extra hardboard on the untrimmed side of the jig so that the saw's motor won't run into clamps during the cut. When you get a new saw blade, retrim one side of the jig so you know the cut line will coincide precisely with the edge of the jig.

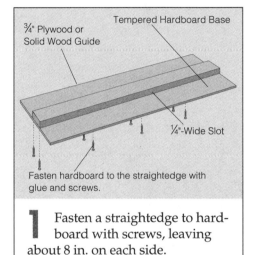

¾" Plywood or Solid Wood Guide

Tempered Hardboard Base

¼"-Wide Slot

Fasten hardboard to the straightedge with glue and screws.

1 Fasten a straightedge to hardboard with screws, leaving about 8 in. on each side.

2 Trim one side of the jig. When cutting plywood with the jig, align the cut end exactly with the cut line on the plywood.

Finishing Edges

One problem with plywood is the appearance of its edges. Most plywoods have voids within their laminations, leaving unsightly gaps visible along the edges. There will be occasions when you'll have to conceal an ugly edge. If the plywood will be painted, you can fill the rough edge and sand it smooth. Otherwise, you can conceal the edge with wood tape or solid-wood edge banding.

Filling an Edge. Thin down latex wood putty with water until it's easily spreadable, then apply it along the edge with a putty knife. After the putty has dried completely, lightly sand the edge with 150-grit sandpaper.

Using Veneer Tape. Most home centers now stock wood veneer tape to match commonly sold plywood panels. Some kinds of wood tape come with pressure-sensitive or heat-activated adhesive so the tape can simply be pressed or ironed onto the edge of the plywood. After the tape is firmly attached to the plywood, lightly sand the edges with 150-grit sandpaper.

Using Solid Wood. You can get a more durable edge that's almost as easy to apply as wood tape simply by gluing solid wood directly onto the edge of the plywood. Screen and half-round molding are both good choices; wider trim will give the appearance of a more substantial panel. You can use masking tape to hold the molding in place while the glue dries. After the glue dries, you can sand or plane the edge flush with the plywood, but it's easier to use a piloted flush-trimming bit in your router.

Making Joints

You can join wood in a variety of ways, ranging from the simple butt joint, to the stronger and more sophisticated dovetail joint, to a whole range of other types of joints that vary in strength and complexity. However, only a few simple joints are called for in the projects in this book: butt, rabbet, dado, and miter joints.

Butt Joint. A butt joint is simply two pieces of wood butted together, edge to face. It's typically secured with glue and some other type of fastener. Although it's a weak joint, it can be easily reinforced. Butt joints are commonly used in face frames where strength is not important because the face-frame members are usually glued to the cabinet. However, face frame butt joints are often reinforced with dowels, which not only add strength but help align the pieces during glue-up.

Miter Joint. A miter joint is an edge-to-edge joint, made by angling the edges. As with butt joints, the miter joint usually requires additional reinforcement with fasteners.

Reinforcing Joints with Dowels

Wood dowels can increase the strength and improve the accuracy of butt joints. The joint includes two dowels glued into the end of one member, then into corresponding holes in the other member.

1 Locating the Dowel Holes. To locate dowel holes accurately, temporarily position the two mating pieces in place. Strike a line on the face of both members, indicating the dowel locations. Transfer

Using Veneer Tape. Attach heat-activated veneer tape by applying a hot iron to the taped edge.

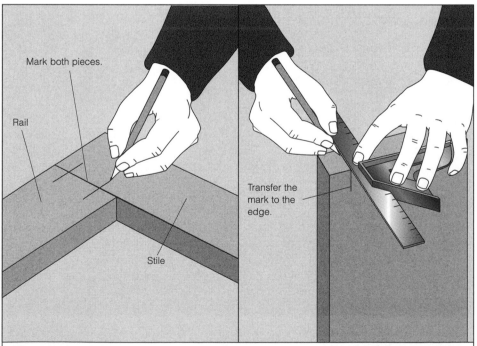

Mark both pieces.

Rail

Stile

Transfer the mark to the edge.

1 Mark the faces of two mating members, and transfer the marks to the edges with a combination square.

those marks onto the edge of each piece with a combination square.

2 Drilling the Holes. Use a doweling jig to ensure that the dowel holes are drilled exactly equidistant from the two faces of the piece. Use a stop collar or a piece of tape on the bit to indicate that you have drilled to the correct depth.

3 Assembling the parts. Apply glue to the dowels and insert them in the holes in one of the parts to be joined. Attach the mating part and clamp the assembly until the glue has set.

Dadoes, Grooves & Rabbets

Dadoes and grooves are identical except that dadoes are actually a type of groove that runs across the grain, and grooves run with the grain. For the sake of clarity, we'll use the term groove to describe only grooves that run with the grain. A rabbet is like a ledge cut along one edge of a piece.

Dadoes are commonly used for fitting shelves and partitions into cabinet panels. Grooves are commonly used for fitting partitions and insetting shelf standards, while rabbets are most often used for joining cabinet panels and insetting cabinet backs.

Making Dadoes & Grooves with a Table Saw

To make dadoes and grooves on a table saw you must use the rip fence. As a result, this method is most suited to making long grooves. For example, this is a handy setup for making grooves for insetting shelf standards. Once you have the fence and blade set up, you can just run panels through, knowing that all your grooves will be equidistant from the panel edges.

You can use the table saw to make dadoes as well, but the longer the panel is, the more awkward this operation will be.

1 Making a Test Cut. Unplug the saw and replace your regular

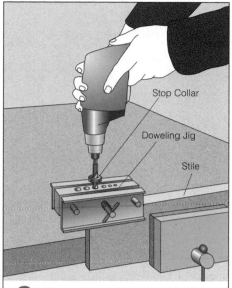

2 Use a doweling jig to drill the holes straight and in the correct positions.

saw blade with a dado cutter. Adjust the cutter for the proper depth of cut and set the fence to the desired distance from the cutter. Before you make the cut on your project, make a test cut in scrap wood to make sure your settings are correct.

Note: When working with a stacked or wobble-type blade, you may need a different throat plate with a wider opening than the one used with an ordinary blade. Once you install the dado head, turn the blade by hand to make sure that it has adequate

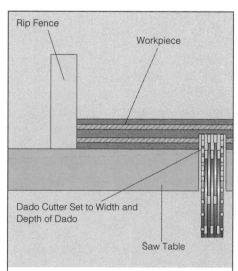

1 Connect a dado cutter to your table saw, set it, then make a test cut.

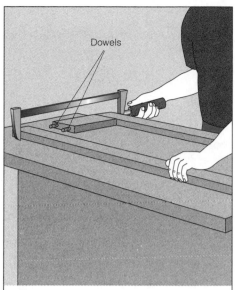

3 Insert glued-up dowels into the holes, then glue, join, and clamp the mating parts.

clearance. If the blade makes contact with the throat plate, you'll have to make a replacement throat plate out of wood. Refer to your saw's instruction manual for directions.

2 Making the Final Cut. To cut the groove or dado in your panel, simply run the panel over the blade and make the cut. Always use push blocks and hold-downs where appropriate to keep the workpiece from lifting off the saw table or kicking back. You can make a feather-

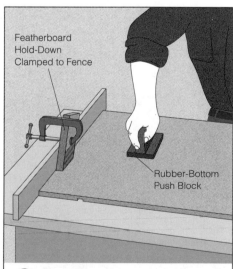

2 Run the panel over the dado blade to make the cut. Always use push blocks and hold-downs.

Making Dadoes and Grooves without a Dado Blade

It's possible to make dadoes and rabbets without a special dado blade. Set up your regular saw blade just as you would a dado head and run the panel over the blade. After the first pass, shut the saw off and move the fence about ⅛ inch from the blade for the second pass. Continue making passes in ⅛-inch increments until the dado or groove is cut to the desired width.

board hold-down simply by kerfing the end of a small board that has had its ends cut on the diagonal. If you need to make a matching dado or groove an opposing panel, be sure you do it before you change the fence adjustment.

Making Rabbets with a Table Saw

Cutting rabbets on the table saw is similar to cutting grooves and dadoes, except that you'll need to equip your saw with an auxiliary wood fence so that the blade can run right up against its edge to accomplish the kind of blade adjustment you'll need for rabbets. Again, because the rip fence is used, this operation is more suitable for cutting rabbets along the edges of long panels than for cutting rabbets along the top or bottom of long panels.

1 **Making the Auxiliary Fence.** Make the auxiliary fence from ¾-inch plywood. Make the fence the same length as and a couple inches higher than the rip fence. Screw the auxiliary fence onto your rip fence. Refer to your owner's manual for instructions. Install the cutter in your saw, and drop the blade below the saw table surface.

2 **Cutting a Blade Cove.** To make the dado cutter easy to adjust, cut a blade cove into the auxiliary fence. With the dado cutter lowered beneath the saw table, move the fence so that it extends over the blade by approximately ⅝ inch, and lock it in place. Make a pencil mark on the left face of the auxiliary fence, 1 inch above the saw table. Turn the saw on, and slowly raise the dado cutter until it hits the pencil mark.

3 **Installing and Adjusting the Cutter.** Set the cutter to the proper blade height, and adjust the auxiliary fence to the desired rabbet width.

4 **Making the Cut.** Make a sample cut on a piece of scrap to check your measurements and saw settings. When the setting is perfect, put the workpiece that you want to rabbet face down on the table and run the piece over the blade.

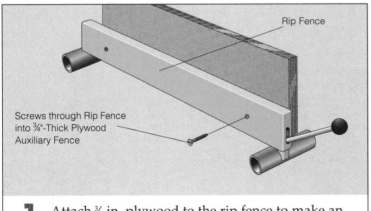

1 Attach ¾-in. plywood to the rip fence to make an auxiliary fence.

- Rip Fence
- Screws through Rip Fence into ¾"-Thick Plywood Auxiliary Fence

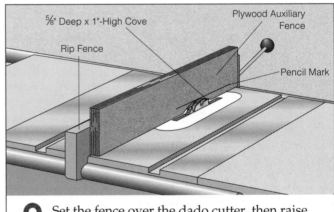

2 Set the fence over the dado cutter, then raise the cutter to create a cove in the fence.

- ⅝" Deep x 1"-High Cove
- Plywood Auxiliary Fence
- Rip Fence
- Pencil Mark

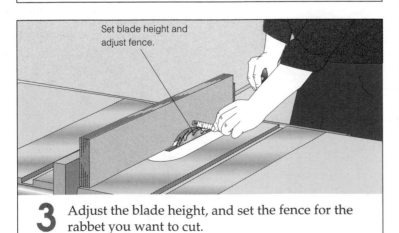

3 Adjust the blade height, and set the fence for the rabbet you want to cut.

- Set blade height and adjust fence.

4 With final adjustments made, run the piece over the cutter to make the rabbet.

- Featherboard Hold-Down Clamped to Fence

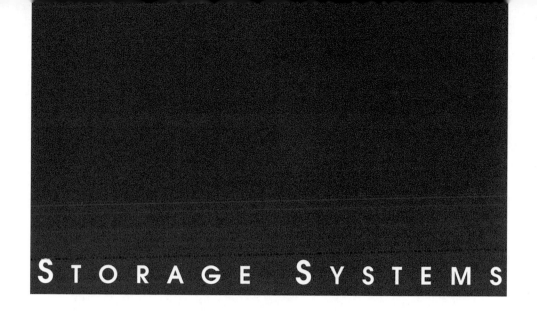

STORAGE SYSTEMS

There are many kinds of manufactured storage systems on the market today, but they all fall into three broad categories: closet organizers made from coated wire, closet organizers made using laminated particleboard, and standard-and-shelf systems. If you want the most storage capacity with the least amount of work, you'll probably be able to find a manufactured system that will fit your needs.

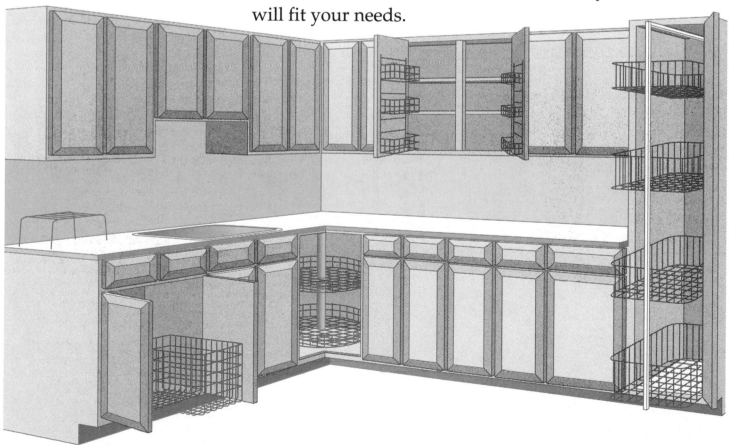

Coated-Wire Frame

Wire-frame storage components have an advantage over other storage units because they're lightweight and inexpensive. They also allow plenty of air circulation. Coated-wire frame systems are easy to install as well. An entire walk-in closet can be set up in a weekend.

Basic Components

Closet-organizing systems are available in stores as individual components that you mix and match yourself to form a unit or as kits that fit certain-size closets. No matter how you buy them, the basic components include uprights, wardrobe shelves with integrated hanging rods, linen shelves without rods, brackets, and back clips. There are also a number of options and accessories.

Shelving. Besides standard shelves with integrated clothes rods, there are shelves with rods that are designed so hangers can slide freely. You can get shelves that round a corner, shelves with oak fascia, tilted shelves for shoes, and corner shelves.

Baskets. Ideal for holding cumbersome items, baskets can be used as part of a closet system, doubling as drawers, or in a stand-alone unit with or without wheels. They can be used individually or grouped, and special under-shelf baskets can double the use of a shelf.

Kitchen Accessories. Coated-wire systems can be used in the kitchen to make cabinetry storage more effective. Some of the units include sliding baskets, caddies, and pantry units; door-mounted racks; Lazy Susans; wastebasket holders; and drawer dividers.

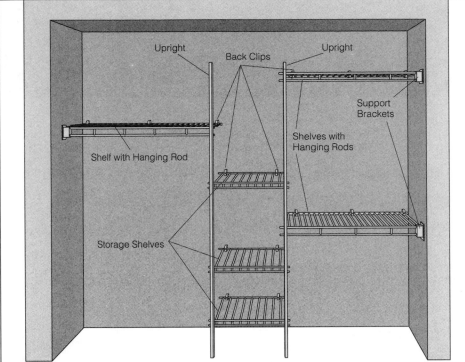

Upright · Back Clips · Upright · Support Brackets · Shelves with Hanging Rods · Shelf with Hanging Rod · Storage Shelves

Basic Components. Coated-wire organizers are easy to install and come in kits to fit standard-size reach-in closets.

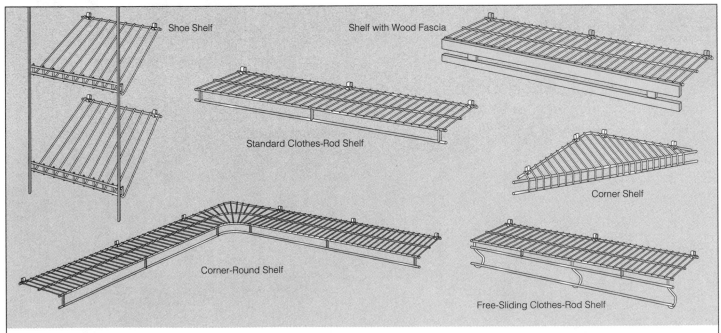

Shoe Shelf · Shelf with Wood Fascia · Standard Clothes-Rod Shelf · Corner Shelf · Corner-Round Shelf · Free-Sliding Clothes-Rod Shelf

Shelving. You can buy coated-wire shelves in a variety of sizes, styles, and configurations.

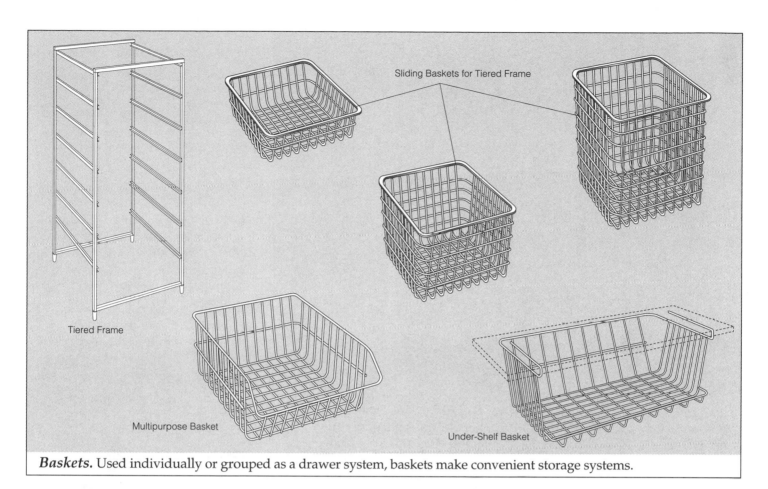

Tiered Frame

Sliding Baskets for Tiered Frame

Multipurpose Basket

Under-Shelf Basket

Baskets. Used individually or grouped as a drawer system, baskets make convenient storage systems.

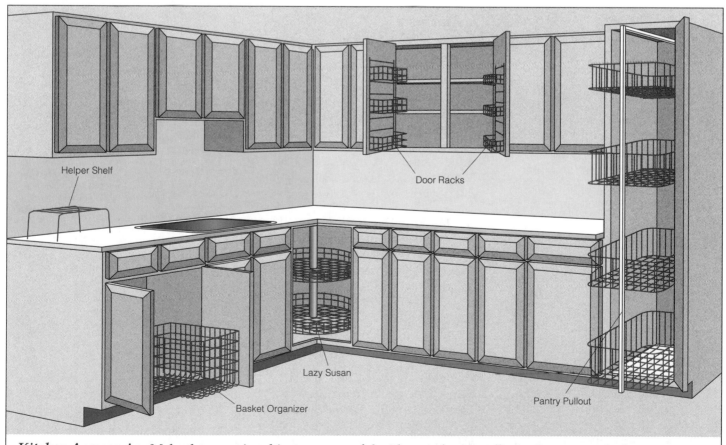

Helper Shelf

Door Racks

Lazy Susan

Basket Organizer

Pantry Pullout

Kitchen Accessories. Make the space in cabinets more useful with coated-wire pullouts, drawers, and other accessories.

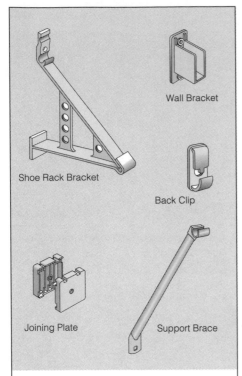

Hardware. Various kinds of brackets, clips, and braces are used to hold coated-wire shelving to the walls.

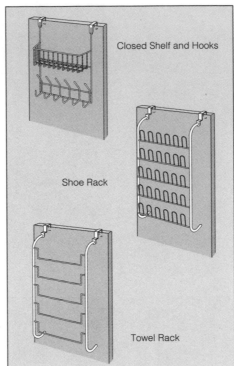

Overdoor Hooks. Hanging off the top edge of a door, these accessories make use of space behind closed closet, pantry, and bathroom doors.

Hardware. There is a small library of hardware required for installed coated-wire systems. Although some minor specifics may vary from manufacturer to manufacturer, the basic principles are the same. Some of the hardware includes wall brackets of various descriptions, support braces, shoe-shelf brackets, joiner plates for joining sections of shelving, back clips (often with built-in wall fasteners), and end caps.

Overdoor Hooks. You can gain extra storage space by using the ordinarily wasted area behind any door with the help of innovative door-hanging shelves, hooks, and baskets. The hanging units attach to the door with metal clips at the top that are sized to the thickness of standard doors. The metal clips are thin enough to fit in the clearance space between the door and the jamb. You can hang and store everything from clothes to cleaning products to household tools.

Installing a Coated-Wire Shelf

Linen shelves and wardrobe shelves with integral clothes rods are installed in basically the same manner. Most coated-wire organizer systems are based on the same general principles, but manufacturers' instructions will vary slightly. Read the instructions carefully before you begin work.

1 Marking the Wall. After you decide where you want the shelf located, measure the height and mark the measurement on the wall at one end. Place a 48-inch level on the mark and draw a line the full length of the shelf. If you don't have a 48-inch level, use a shorter level and a straightedge.

2 Cutting the Shelf. Subtract 1½ inches from the shelf length if the shelf will abut a wall at both ends. Subtract ¾ inch if the shelf will abut a wall at one end. Use the full length if the shelf will not

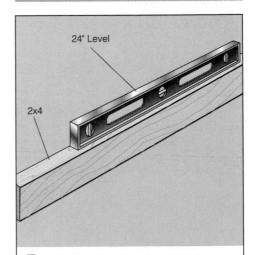

1 Use a 48-in. level or a 24-in. level and a straightedge to mark the shelf location on the wall.

abut a wall. Cut the shelf to length with bolt cutters. Slide plastic end caps over the ends of all the wires.

3 **Installing the Clips.** Start 2½ inches from one end of the shelf if you're installing it against a wall and 1 inch if not. Place a vertical mark above the shelf line and additional marks every 12 inches or 10 inches if the shelf is less than 48 inches long. Put a final mark at 2½ inches from the opposite wall or 1 inch short of the total length if the end of the shelf is open. At each mark, measure ⅝ inch above the shelf line and make a horizontal line to form a cross. For hollow walls, drill a ¼-inch hole at the center of each cross. If you hit a stud, use a ⁵⁄₃₂-inch bit.

For hollow walls, tap a back clip and fastener into each hole and drive a screw, holding the clip with the other hand. To fasten the clip to solid-wood wall studs, use a plain back clip and a screw.

4 **Installing the Shelf.** Place the back of the shelf just above the clips in the wall. For longer shelves you may need two people, one to hold the shelf in place and the other to set the shelf into the clips. Starting at one end, snap the back wire of the shelf into the clips by setting the shelf vertically on the groove in the clips and tapping the front of the shelf with your hand. It should snap into place without too much force. Work one clip at a time until you reach the other end.

5 **Installing an End Bracket.** For all shelf ends that abut a wall, you'll need an end bracket to anchor the shelf. Lower the shelf and level the end at the wall. Slide the end bracket onto the shelf. Use a pencil to mark the mounting holes in the bracket onto the wall. Lift the shelf out of the way, and drill a ¼-inch hole at each mark. Insert the plastic anchor in each hole, set

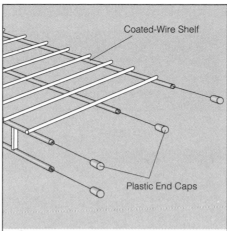

2 Cut the shelving with bolt cutters and cover the ends with plastic end caps.

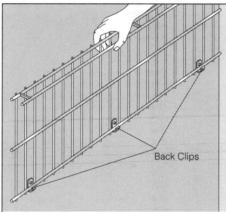

4 Hold the shelf vertically above the back clips, then snap the back wire into place on each clip.

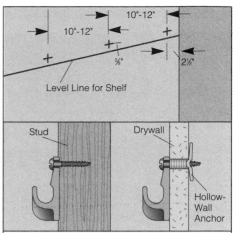

3 Measure, mark, and attach the back clips to the wall. Screw directly into studs or use hollow-wall anchors.

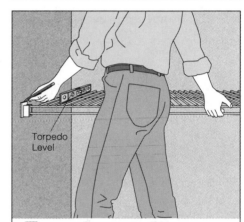

5 Insert an end bracket on the shelf, level the shelf, and mark the screw holes. Attach the bracket and snap the shelf in place.

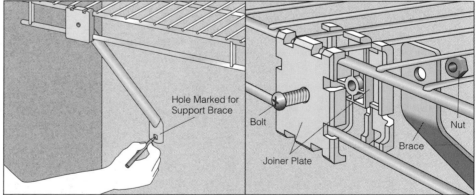

6 Screw the bottom of a support brace to the wall, then attach the brace to the shelf with a joiner plate.

the end bracket in place, and secure the bracket with a screw in each mounting hole. Lower the shelf again, and snap it into the end bracket.

6 **Installing a Support Brace.** You'll need to install support braces every 42 inches along a shelf and at shelf ends that don't butt a wall. Attach two back clips to the shelf, one right-side up and one upside down, at each support-brace location. Place joiner plates on the lip of the shelf at each location as well. Turn the plates vertically for an integral rod and shelf and horizontally for linen shelves. Insert a joiner-plate bolt through the plates from the front. Place the smaller end of the support brace over the bolt at the rear, thread a nut onto the bolt, and hand-tighten it.

Level the shelf in place and mark the location of the support brace's lower hole. Pivot the shelf upward, and drill a ¼-inch hole at each brace-hole mark. Insert a plastic anchor, lower the shelf, and fasten the support brace with a screw. Tighten the bolt and nut that holds the top end of the support brace on the joiner plate. Some systems snap into place on the front of the shelf rather than using joiner plates.

Laminated Particleboard

Solid laminated storage systems are made with a plastic surface material laminated to particleboard. Because particleboard can chip easily, be careful when installing screws or making any hardware connections. Particleboard is also heavy; you'll probably need help lifting and installing completed laminated components.

Components

Panels. The units are made of vertical panels and a series of fixed shelves, which give the structure rigidity. The vertical panels create the sides of a storage unit and come in two varieties: end panels and center panels. End panels have holes drilled on the left or right side; you use them to create the end sides of a shelf or drawer tower. Adjoining units share a center

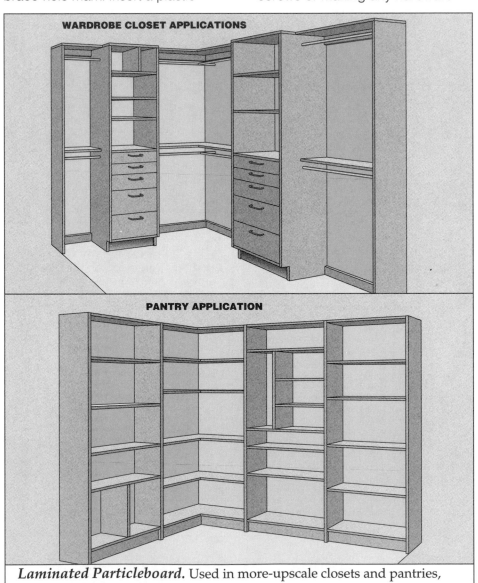

Laminated Particleboard. Used in more-upscale closets and pantries, particleboard storage systems cost more than wire units and give more of a furniture-quality appearance.

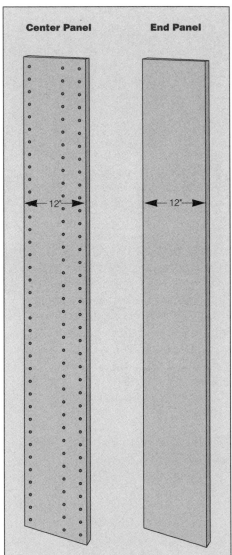

Panels. Center panels have holes for shelves drilled in both sides; end panels have holes in only one side.

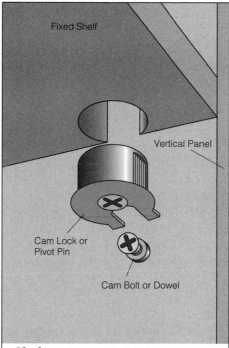

Shelves. Fixed shelves connect to panels with locking fasteners.

panel, which has holes drilled on both sides.

Shelves. Fixed shelves connect two vertical panels, determining the width of the unit and imparting structural rigidity. The shelves attach to the panels with locking and alignment fasteners.

Other Parts. Drawers come in a variety of widths and heights. They are normally precut for quick install-ation and come with all necessary hardware. Baskets can also be fitted into the units, as can solid-panel shelf dividers, which separate the shelf area into two or three compart-ments. Doors and kickboards are also available to give a finished look to units in large walk-in closets, pantries, and the like.

Note: Since different manufacturers have slightly different fastening syst-

ems, most of which are patented, alw-ays follow their installation procedures.

Securing a Laminated Shelf Tower

Measure and mark the desired location for the shelf and/or drawer tower in the closet. Use a level to draw a plumb line at the mark. Set the shelf tower in place in the closet against the vertical line. Hold an angle bracket in place on one side, near the top. Mark the hole locations on the shelf tower and the back closet wall. Repeat on the other side, then remove the tower. At each of the four marks on the closet back wall, drill a hole to accommodate the hollow-wall anchors you're using, and insert an anchor into each hole. Set the tower back into place, secure angle brackets on each side to

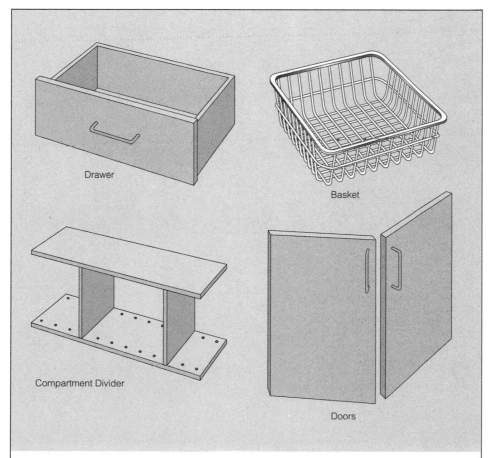

Other Parts. Accessories for fixed laminated-particleboard storage systems include drawers, baskets, shelf compartment dividers, and doors to make the units look more like built-in furniture.

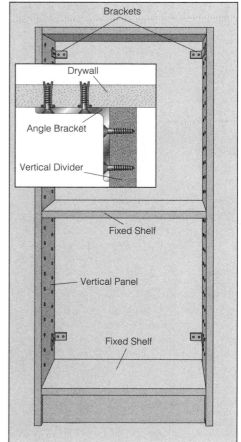

Securing a Laminated Shelf Tower. Use angle brackets or other supplied fasteners to secure a laminated system.

the wall with 1-inch screws, then attach each bracket to the tower with ¾-inch screws.

Standard & Shelf Systems

Metal shelf standards are usually made of steel and come in a variety of finishes. Standard lengths range from 12 to 144 inches and can be cut with a hacksaw to fit any requirements. They are surface-mounted to walls with screws. If the shelves will hold a heavy load like books, try to attach at least one of the standards to wall studs for the best support. Shelf brackets fit into slots located about every ½ inch, so you can adjust the shelves quickly and easily.

Hanging the Shelves

1 Installing the First Standard. Decide on the amount of overhang you want at each end of the shelving, then use the remainder as the space between the standards. Locate the position of the standards on the wall, making sure at least one standard is over a stud. Plumb one of the standards on the wall, and mark the side of the standard as well as a mounting hole. Drill a hole for the fastener, and drive the screw barely tight enough to hold the standard in place. Plumb the standard again, drill the remaining mounting holes, and fasten the standard.

2 Finishing the Job. Hold the second standard so the mounting holes line up with the first standard. Set one bracket in the first standard and another in the second standard in the corresponding slots. Hold the second standard in its place on the wall and lay a 48-inch-long level across the brackets until it reads level. Mark the mounting holes for the second standard, drill holes for the fasteners, and mount the standard. Set the brackets in place and lay in the shelves, making sure they're aligned properly.

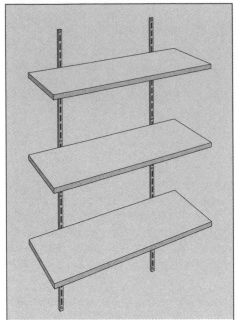

Standard-and-Shelf Systems. For quick and easy—yet sturdy—shelving, attach metal standards to the wall and use adjustable brackets that hold shelves.

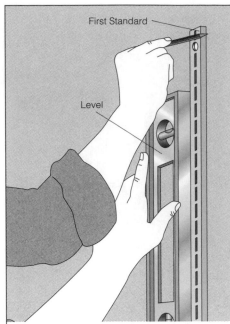

1 Plumb and mark the position of the first standard. After you attach the top screw, make sure the standard is plumb, then drill for the rest of the screws.

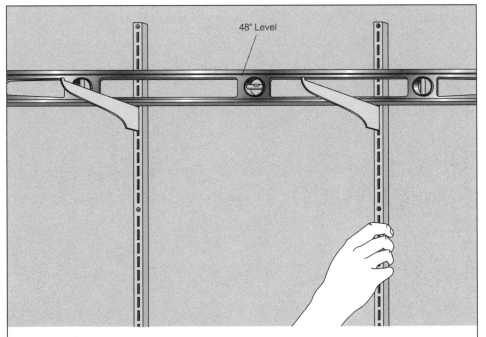

2 To position the other standard, lay a 48-in. level across two similarly positioned brackets and adjust the loose standard until it reads level.

Decorative Standards

Some shelf-and-standard systems use decorative covers to disguise their utilitarian purpose. The standard covers, end caps, decorative brackets, and accessories like fitted bookends give the shelves a designer look and hide all the fastening hardware so the shelves appear more like built-in units. These shelves usually come in kits, complete with an installation template.

KITCHEN & PANTRY STORAGE

The kitchen, which in part is designed with storage in mind, is the one area in your house that you may think has adequate storage. But look closely and follow the advice in this chapter, and you'll be able to increase the utility and efficiency of your kitchen.

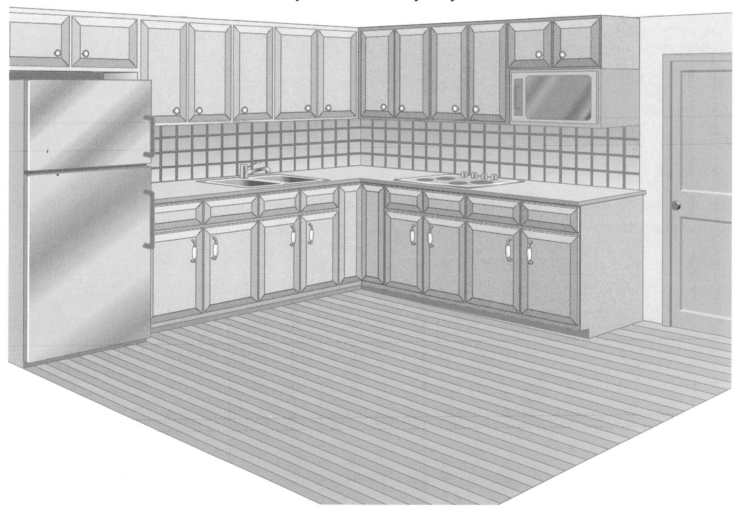

Existing Cabinet Alterations

A look into any kitchen cupboard or pantry will often reveal plenty of empty space. You can make use of spare space by altering existing cabinetry with manufactured accessories or by building similar components yourself. The following suggestions will help you put space to work.

Making a Tilt-Out Soap Tray

Sponges, steel-wool pads, soap bars, scrubbing brushes, and the like inevitably find their way to the kitchen countertop alongside the sink. Besides crowding the area around the sink, these cleaning aids are unsightly. If your sink base cabinet has a false drawer-front panel, you can create a handy storage space for these accessories using a tilt-out tray designed to hold sponges and the like. The trays, which come in plastic and stainless-steel versions, are available at home centers and hardware stores.

1 Removing the False Panel.
Most false drawer fronts are fastened by screwed-on battens inside the cabinet. Open the sink-base doors to gain access to the inside of the cabinet and remove the screws to free the false panel. Be careful not to damage the panel because it will become the front of the tilt-out storage hatch.

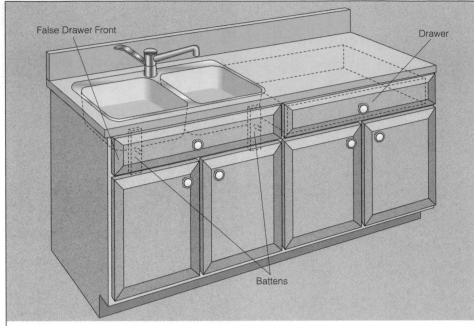

Making a Tilt-Out Soap Tray. Most sink bases have a false front, attached by battens from the rear. Use this panel to make a hidden soap tray.

If you discover that the drawer front is nailed to the base cabinet instead of screwed on, use caution when removing it. Run a utility knife along the front perimeter. This will help break the bond between the sink base and the drawer front. Free the panel with a few hammer blows from behind. When you've removed the drawer front, don't tap the nails out. Instead, pull them through with a pair of pliers from behind. Tapping them through the front face can cause a splinter or chip in the face. Pulling the nail from the rear will at worst leave only a nail-hole in front. Often no hole is left.

2 Attaching the Tray. Most tilt-out trays provide hanging slots so that once the tray is installed, it can be removed and cleaned. When you fasten the tray, be sure the screws are short enough so that they don't puncture the finished face.

3 Installing the Hardware.
Fasten the tilt-out hinges to the sides of the cabinet stile and the tray. Hinges from various manu-

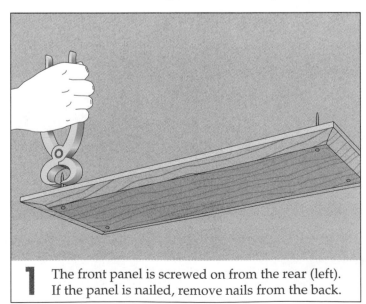

1 The front panel is screwed on from the rear (left). If the panel is nailed, remove nails from the back.

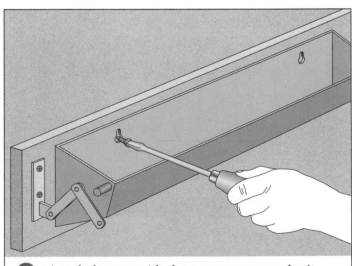

2 Attach the tray with short screws so you don't puncture the panel's face.

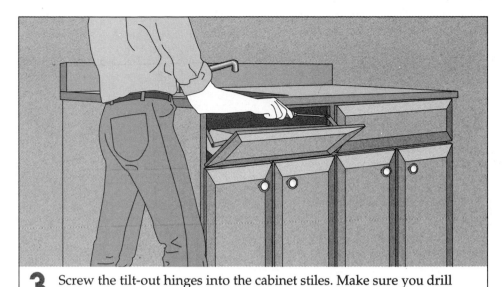

3 Screw the tilt-out hinges into the cabinet stiles. Make sure you drill pilot holes before installing the screws to avoid splitting the wood.

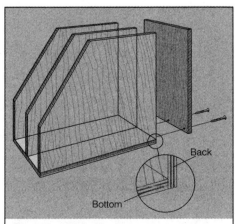

¾"x¾" Block Fastened to Cabinet Floor

Drawer Slides

Installing Roll-Out Tray Dividers. Create vertical storage for trays and such with plywood and drawer slides. You can take up the entire cabinet space or just half of it.

facturers may differ in installation procedures, so check your particular hardware.

Installing Roll-Out Tray Dividers

Storing large shallow pans, cutting boards, and cookie sheets, especially large ones, is a challenge. These items are ordinarily placed at the bottom of a stack of pots and pans because they're so big. This arrangement poses an access problem because getting to the bottom of the stack requires that you take out the other items first. You can solve this problem by creating vertical storage space with a roll-out rack.

Using a pair of common full-extension drawer slides, a slab of ¾-inch plywood, and a 24-inch-long block of ¾ x ¾-inch wood (ripped from a 1x2), you can build a handy roll-out rack.

1 **Building the Roll-Out Unit.**
Cut two slabs of ¾-inch plywood to the appropriate size. The size will depend on your cabinet's width. Set the back slab behind the bottom slab and fasten it with screws. Cut the tray dividers from the same-size stock. The dividers will provide individual slots for storage and make the unit stiffer and more stable. You can vary the space between dividers according to your needs. About 2 inches is a good average width.

Back

Bottom

1 Cut the unit pieces from ¾-in. plywood and assemble them with screws.

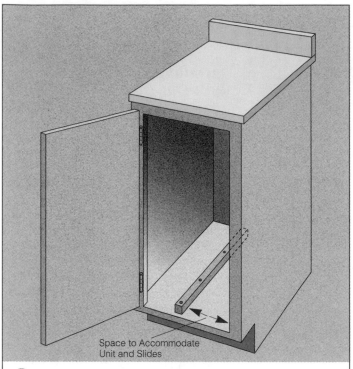

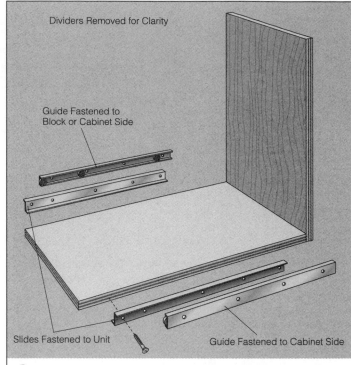

2 If you're not taking up the whole cabinet, screw blocking to the cabinet floor at the desired width.

3 Attach the drawer slides to the roll-out unit and the guides to the cabinet and blocking if you're using it.

2 Providing Blocking for the Drawer Slides. A roll-out doesn't have to occupy the entire cabinet unless the cabinet is narrow (12 inches or so). If you have a cabinet that's 15 inches wide or more, you can use ¾ x ¾-inch blocking to allow you to isolate part of the base cabinet as free space and part of it as a roll-out tray divider. With wood or buglehead screws, affix the blocking to the floor of the cabinet parallel to a side wall. The blocking should be placed at a distance that will accommodate both the width of the roll-out divider unit and the drawer slides. Standard drawer slides need approximately ½ inch of clearance.

3 Installing Drawer Slides. Fasten the drawer slides to both sides of the roll-out unit, then affix the corresponding guides, one to the inside of the blocking and one to the cabinet wall. Once you've attached all the sliding hardware to the cabinet and the divider, roll the unit onto the guides and test it. If the fit is too tight or too loose, adjust it by moving the blocking.

Assembling Circular Shelves

Corner cabinets have deep recesses compared with regular cabinets, so items placed in the rear of these cabinets are difficult to reach. Rotating circular shelves make it easy to get at all items in the cabinet. Although there is technically less storage space around a circular shelf, the ease of access more than compensates for the slight loss of space.

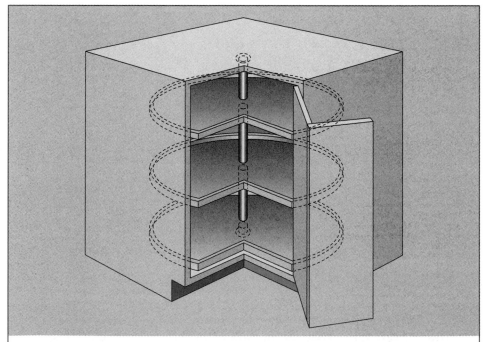

Assembling Circular Shelves. It's difficult to make use of the rear space in corner cabinets. Circular shelves make the space accessible.

A typical rotating circular shelf kit consists of two or three circular shelves, top and bottom flanges, a center support rod, and disk-like hubs to support each shelf. The hardware is difficult to purchase separately, so you're better off buying a manufactured unit or kit. For corner cabinets that have a 90-degree inside corner, there are circular rotating shelves that have a "pie slice" wedge missing to fit around the inside corner.

1 Locating the Center Point.
Place one of the shelves inside an empty cabinet, then check clearances around the shelf. Locate the center point of the unit. With a level or plumb bob, transfer this point to the ceiling of the cabinet, then to the bottom of the cabinet. Using the center point as a reference, fasten the top flange to the cabinet top or ceiling. It may be that the ceiling of the cabinet is actually the bottom of your countertop. If this is the case, be sure not to screw too deeply into the countertop or you will penetrate the surface.

2 Installing the Center Pole and Shelves.
Check the length of the center pole against the height inside the cabinet, and using a hacksaw, cut the pole to fit. Assemble the shelves, together with their corresponding hubs and the bottom flange, outside the cabinet. Tilt the assembly into the secured flange at the top, and locate the bottom flange over the bottom center point. Fasten the bottom flange in place, checking for plumb, and adjust the height of the shelves.

1 Transfer the center point of the rotating unit inside the cabinet using a plumb bob.

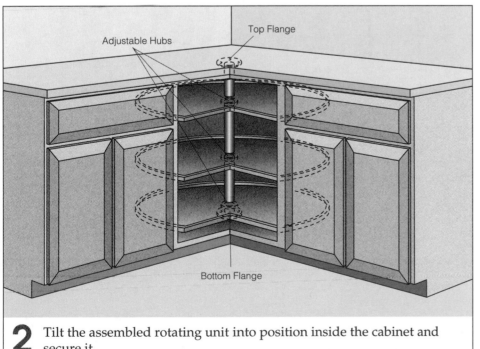

Adjustable Hubs

Top Flange

Bottom Flange

2 Tilt the assembled rotating unit into position inside the cabinet and secure it.

Making Recycling Bins

Recycling, it seems, has become part of modern everyday life. Whatever your commitment to recycling, it helps to have efficient storage like rotating bins that go under the counter and out of the way. The same design and procedures for installing circular shelves can be used to make handy rotating bins for recyclables, except that you'll replace the circular shelves with a three-bin turning carousel. You can use one bin for plastics, another for aluminum and other metal, and the third for glass.

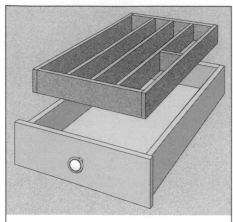

Making Kitchen Utensil Organizers. Make a simple butt-joint drawer organizer from plywood or one-by stock. ●

Making Kitchen Utensil Organizers

Drawers, especially those that hold kitchen utensils, can quickly become disorganized. You can buy a manu-factured organizer made from plastic, but it may not suit your needs—and it may not be adjustable. It's better to build your own organizer, made to your own specifications. Use ½- or ¾-inch plywood strips or solid-wood stock cut to the height of the existing drawer walls. Since styles of utensils vary in size and shape, use the uten-sils you'll store in that drawer to de-sign the openings between dividers. Make the compartments at least ¾ inch longer than the actual utensils and three times the width. Keeping the unit square, glue and fasten all the components. Use two screws to attach the insert to the drawer from underneath. The screws will prevent the insert from sliding back and forth as it's opened and closed.

Installing Door Racks

Much of the wasted space in a cabi-net may be located directly behind the cabinet door. The best way to make use of this space is to install easy-to-build door racks, as long as the doors have no shelves behind them or the shelves are at least 4 inches from the door. Door-mounted shelves are ideal for pantries and under-sink cabinets, where they can store soaps, cleansers, and other cleaning paraphernalia.

Measure the back of the cabinet door and subtract at least ½ inch on all sides to clear the cabinet face frame. Cut a slab of ¾-inch-thick plywood to this size for the rear support panel. Cut the side panels from one-by solid wood 3½ inches wide and the height of the support panel. Cut the shelves and shelf stops from one-by stock as well, but rip the stops to ¼ inch thick or use ¼-inch plywood. Keep in mind that the shelves must be wide and deep enough to fit into the dadoes of the sides and rear support panel.

Lay the rear support panel and side panels on a worktable, clamp them together, and plow dadoes through them (see page 21). Doing this will en-sure that the dadoes of all three sections will align when assembled.

Round or bevel the top outside edge of the side panels to avoid sharp 90-degree corners.

Squeeze glue into the dadoes of the rear support panel, place the shelves into the grooves, and nail them with 4d finishing nails through the back of the unit. Put glue into the dadoes of the side support panels, and tap them onto the shelves. Nail accordingly, checking that the unit is square. Affix the shelf stops using a dab of glue and one 4d finishing nail per side.

Using 1¼-inch wood or drywall screws, fasten the rack to the rear of the cabinet door. Clamp the rack to the door, and drill pilot holes through the unit and partially into the door. Pilot holes are especially important if your cabinet door is made from a hardwood like oak, ash, maple, or birch.

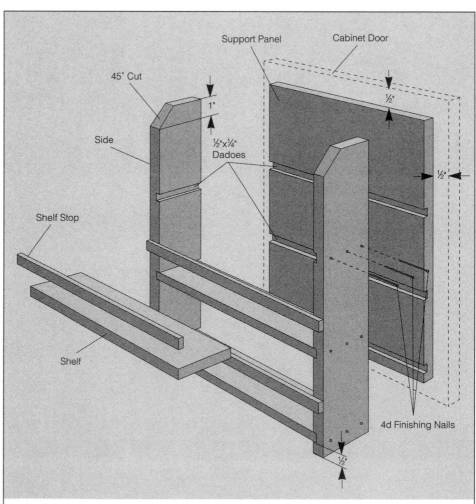

Installing Door Racks. Attach shelves made from plywood and one-by stock to the backs of cabinet doors for extra storage.

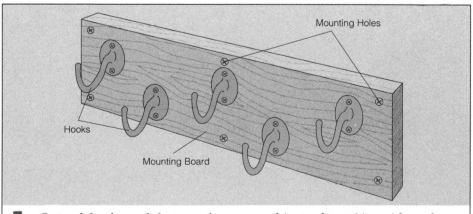

Hanging Pots, Pans, and Cookware. Look around your kitchen for space to install a rack for hanging cookware.

Mounting Holes

Hooks

Mounting Board

1 Cut a slab of wood that matches your cabinets about 6 in. wide and as long as you need, but at least 16 in. Also select decorative hooks.

Hangers & Racks

Sometimes the best place to store something is in plain sight. You can build simple hangers and racks of various sorts that will keep your cookware, wine, and stemware readily available yet out of the way.

Hanging Pots, Pans & Cookware

Style permitting, a handy place to keep pots, pans, and other cookware is on hooks hung around the kitchen work area, perhaps near the range or cooktop. This is a good example of "form following function."

1 **Preparing the Mounting Board.** Select a mounting board to correspond with the species of wood your cabinets are made from. The stock should be at least ¾ inch thick and 4 to 6 inches wide. The length is insignificant, since the board will be anchored to the wall studs at 16-inch intervals. Stain and finish the board to match the existing cabinetry.

Select decorative hooks to match your kitchen and cabinetry style. Keeping the size of your cookware in mind, arrange the hooks in an alternating up-and-down pattern and fasten them to the board screws.

2 **Mounting the Assembled Unit.** If you're attaching the board to

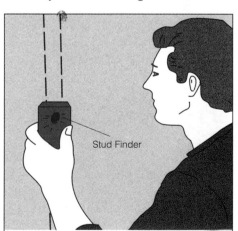

Stud Finder

2 If you're attaching the rack to the side of a cabinet, install it with at least two screws. To fasten the rack to a wall, find studs as attachment points.

a wall, locate and mark the studs with a stud finder. Keep in mind the height of the unit so that the cookware will be in easy reach of everyone who's going to use it. Of course, if you're attaching the board to a cabinet end panel, you don't have to worry about studs. Drill and countersink the mounting holes, then fasten the board with 2-inch screws on ½-inch drywall and 1¼-inch screws on wood.

Building Bottle Racks

In terms of storage-space efficiency, the best way to store bottles of wine is to stand them upright on a shelf in rows. According to wine experts, however, the bottles should be horizontal and slightly tilted, so that the cork is immersed in the liquid, to preserve the quality of the wine during storage. This tilt calls for a pitch of approximately 10 degrees, depending on the shape of the bottle, which will ensure against the cork's drying and shrinking—and the spoiling of the contents. Hanging a wine rack under a wall cabinet will at least free up some space in the cupboards above and make wine storage more efficient.

1 Cutting the Parts. Using veneered plywood, cut the five sections as shown. The front, back, and sides should all be ripped to a height of 5½ inches. The top section should be ripped to a depth of 6 inches. The width of your rack can vary depending on your preference. The drawing shows a five-bottle rack 23½ inches wide. This width can be increased or decreased by adding to or subtracting from the unit by increments of 4½ inches. A four-bottle rack, for example, would be 19 inches wide (23½ - 4½ = 19).

2 Laying Out the Openings. Using the guidelines mentioned in Step 1, draw a horizontal guideline through the center of both front and back components. Under the center line of the rear component, draw another line parallel to it 1 inch away. Make sure your pencil lines are extremely faint so they can easily be sanded away when finishing.

Measuring from left to right on the front section, put a vertical mark through the horizontal line at

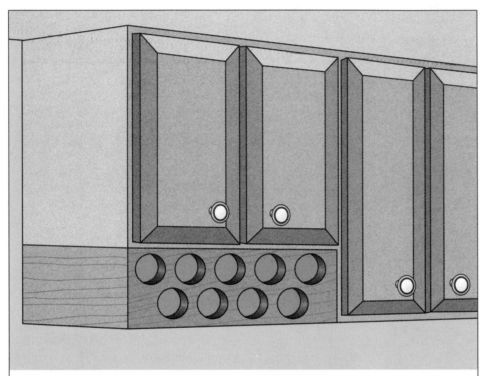

Building Bottle Racks. Make a wine rack from hardwood plywood and install it under a cabinet in the kitchen.

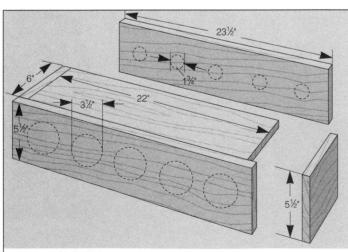

1 Cut the parts using unit dimensions as guidelines. The overall width will depend on your cabinetry.

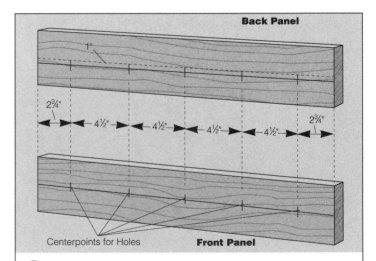

2 Draw centerlines on the front and back panels. Measure down 1 in. on the back. Make vertical marks on each panel as shown.

2¾ inches from the edge, then put consecutive vertical marks at 4½-inch increments accordingly.

On the rear section, again measuring from left to right, put a vertical mark through the off-center horizontal line at 2¾ inches from the edge, then put vertical consecutive marks at 4½-inch increments accordingly. These will be the center marks for the bottle holes.

3 **Cutting the Holes.** Using an electric drill, bore pilot holes through the center marks on both the front and rear sections. Accurate pilot holes will ensure that the larger holes will align. Insert a 3½ inch hole saw into your power drill. Carefully cut the front holes. Then use a smaller 1¾-inch hole saw to cut the rear holes.

4 **Assembling the Parts.** Assemble the parts so that the side sections are between the front and rear sections. The top section should be between the side sections and the front and rear pieces. Clamp, glue, and fasten the pieces together using 6d finishing nails. Allow the glue to dry overnight, then finish the unit accordingly.

5 **Hanging the Rack.** As a rule of thumb, use nuts and bolts to hang various racks, appliances, radios, and other such under-the-cabinet units; wood screws are less reliable for fastening such items. Also, the sharp tips of such screws can penetrate the bottom shelf. Drill holes in the top of the unit, then hold it in place and mark the hole locations on the bottom of the cabinet. Depending on the width, four to six holes will be appropriate. Drill the holes in the cabinet bottom. Position the rack, slip bolts through the holes,

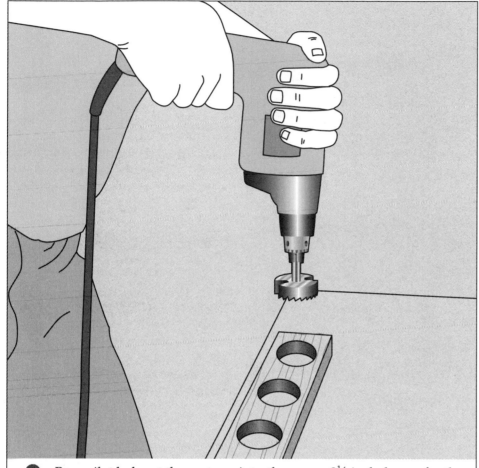

3 Bore pilot holes at the centerpoints, then use a 3½-in. hole saw for the font holes and a 1¾-in. hole saw for the back.

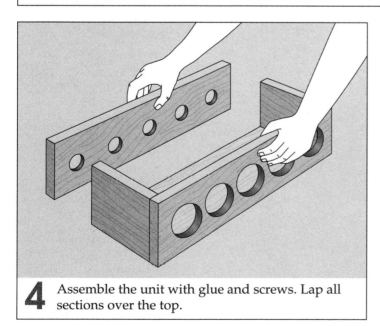

4 Assemble the unit with glue and screws. Lap all sections over the top.

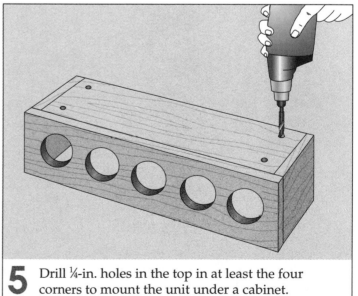

5 Drill ¼-in. holes in the top in at least the four corners to mount the unit under a cabinet.

and tighten the bolts with nuts and washers. The length of the bolts will depend on the thickness of the cabinet; the diameter should be at least ¼ inch.

Note: When installing the wine rack in the kitchen, take care not to hang it over heated areas like a rear-cooled refrigerator or oven. Heat can alter the quality and consistency of wine.

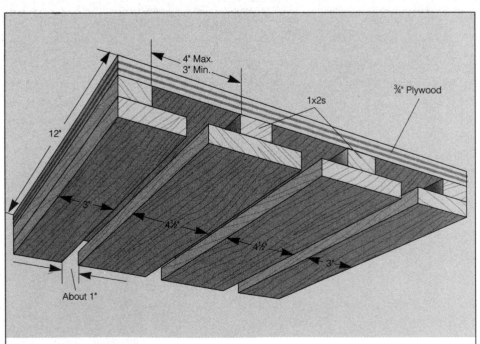

Stemware Hanger. Be sure to mount the stemware hanger out of the way of smoke and grease.

Making the Hanger. The distance between spacers should be no more than 4 in. and no less than 3 in.

Stemware Hanger

Instead of storing stemware inside a cabinet, you can hang it under a cabinet. A stemware hanger is easy to build; however, placement of the unit is an important concern. Place the unit away from smoke and dust. Rising smoke and grease from the stove, deep fryer, waffle iron, and the like, or smoke from cigarettes will deposit on the inside of the upside-down stemware. You'd have to constantly wipe your stemware clean before using it.

Making the Hanger. Using ¾-inch plywood, cut one large slab that will be the mounting board for the entire unit. Cut the board to the same depth as the wall cabinet from which it will hang, usually 12 inches. The width can vary. The edges can be veneer-taped or faced with solid wood to hide the cross plies. Make the spacer slats from 1x2s and the bottom rails from one-by solid stock. Cut the end rails to a width of 3 inches and the middle rails to 4½ inches. Cut the length of the slats and rails to the same depth as the mounting board.

The measurements between spacer slats will vary according to how wide you've decided to make your hanger. As a rule, the distance between spacers should be no wider than 4 inches and no less than 3 inches. First glue and nail the spacer slats to the plywood top with 4d finishing nails. Next, screw the bottom rails through the spacer slats to the mounting board. Provide a gap between bottom rails of about 1 inch.

Predrill holes in the unit, then hold the unit in place and drill through the bottom of the cabinet. Slip appropriate-sized carriage bolts (depending on your cabinet's thickness) through holes with washers on either side, and tighten. Provide four such fasteners.

CLOSET STORAGE

The standards and suggestions in this chapter will help you design and organize your own closets, maximizing space and convenience. These standards can be applied to the installation of either manufactured components or custom-built units.

Standard Closet Specifications

Sometimes it is difficult to design something when you are unsure where things belong. The following are some traditional closet standards.

Standard Closets

Reach-in Closet. The conventional bedroom clothes closet should be at least 24 inches deep and, for each person using it, a minimum of 60 inches wide.

Coat Closet. Closets intended to hold outerwear should be deeper than a regular clothing closet—26 to 30 inches deep. The center of the hanging pole should be 13 to 15 inches from the rear wall. This extra depth provides air circulation to dry damp and musty outerwear. Always locate these closets near the most-used entrance to the house.

Linen Closet. Linen closets require no hanging space, so they don't have to be as deep as clothes closets. A typical linen closet can be 16 to 20 inches deep by 24 inches wide. Shelves should run from floor to ceiling at 12 to 18 inches from one another. The first shelf should be slightly higher from the floor—perhaps 24 inches—to accommodate storage boxes or seasonal linens. These closets should be centrally located near bathrooms and bedrooms.

Poles

Single Pole. When a closet has only one hanging pole, the pole should be approximately 64 inches from the floor. For handicapped accessibility, the maximum height from the floor is 54 inches. The center of the pole should be at least 12 inches from the rear wall.

Double Poles. Two hanging poles should be arranged so that the bottom pole is 36 inches from the floor and the top one is about 70 inches high. Both pole centers should be at least 12 inches from the rear wall.

Pole Length. For a clothing closet, there should be 5 linear feet of hanging pole for one person, 10 linear feet for two. One linear foot of hanging pole can accommodate five to six business suits, twice that many shirts, six dresses and/or pants, or four to five coats.

Shelves

Hat Shelf. A shelf above a hanging pole, traditionally called a hat shelf, should be 2 to 3 inches above the pole and 12 to 18 inches deep. If height permits, subsequent shelving should be 12 to 18 inches above this first shelf. Shelves used by children or shorter adults should be installed at about the top of their heads.

Clothing Shelves. Compartment shelving for folded clothing should have a clear opening of 12 to 18 inches in height, 12 inches in width, and 14 inches in depth. Similar compartment shelving for shoe boxes should be 6 inches high, 9 inches wide, and 12 to 14 inches deep.

Other Closet Features

Wall Mirror. The top of a dressing mirror should be 80 to 84 inches from the floor. The back side of a closet door is a convenient place to hang a dressing mirror.

Counter Height. Custom-built dressing counters can be taller than traditional cabinetry, which is approxi-

Shelves (Cross Section)

Rod (Cross Section)

12"-18"

2"-3"

12"

12"

Hanging Rods (Cross Section)

70"

12"

62"-63"

42"-48"

36"

Standard Closet Specifications. Follow these time-tested guidelines for convenient storage when building a closet or installing an organizing system.

mately 24 inches tall. Dressers can vary according to the user's height, to a maximum of 42 to 48 inches from the floor.

Hooks and Racks. Hooks can be fastened at any height; however, avoid hooks at eye level because they can be dangerous. Also avoid putting hooks in children's rooms. The back side of a door is a good place for hooks and racks, but be careful not to overload such a door because you may loosen its hinges.

Doors. The doors to a closet can help or hinder the closet's usefulness. Pocket doors, when they're open, leave the opening unencumbered and provide full accessibility to the inside of the closet. But pocket doors are infamous for going off their tracks. From a practical point of view, a swing door is best. Accessibility is comparable with a pocket door, with the compromise of the wall space you give up when the door is open. Bifold doors provide between 50 and 75 percent accessibility, while sliders give you only 50 percent accessibility.

Designing a Walk-in Closet

Theoretically, a walk-in closet can be any size. Since space is usually limited, however, a walk-in closet should make an efficient use of space. The following layout makes efficient use of space and accessibility.

Dimensions and Layout. Keeping in mind that hanging storage occupies a depth of 24 inches and that 5 linear feet satisfy the needs of the average person, a walk-in-closet efficiently designed for two people can minimally be 7 feet wide by 6 feet deep (see drawing below). This might include double hanging poles on one side with a shelf above, while on the other side would be a single pole with a series of two to three shelves above. At the back of the closet you should place a combination shelf and drawer unit for small articles of clothing not suitable for hanging or storing on shelves, such as socks, undergarments, shorts, handkerchiefs, and the like.

Doors: Placement and Accessibility. Note in the diagram that the door is located in the center of the closet. The center is the most efficient place to locate a door in a closet like this because it doesn't compromise storage space. Notice also that the door swings out, not into the closet. Doors usually swing into a room to avoid the possibility of hitting someone outside the room with a swinging door. An exception can be made for walk-in closets because there is minimal traffic around them.

Shelves for Folded Clothing

A simple modular shelf unit can be used in any walk-in closet to store a large assortment of folded clothing. What makes shelf storage superior to traditional drawer storage is its ease of access and ease of viewing. You can literally see every stored item at one glance.

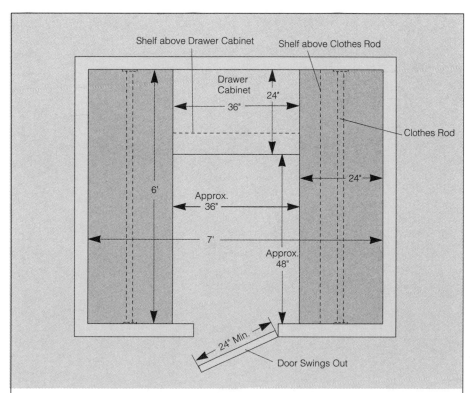

Designing a Walk-in Closet. The ideal walk-in closet for two takes up about 42 sq. ft., with hanging areas on both sides and a drawer or shelf tower in the middle.

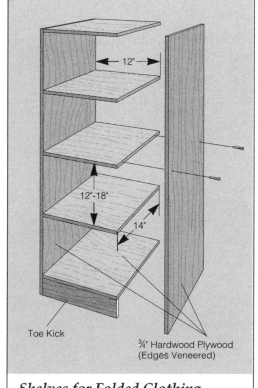

Shelves for Folded Clothing. A tower provides ideal storage for folded sweaters and shirts.

Building the Shelf Unit

This shelf unit is extremely simple to make. It's made entirely of ¾-inch plywood veneered at its visible edges. The unit is 80 inches high, as shown, but you can make it any height you'd like as long as you maintain the 12-inch width, which accommodates folded sweaters and pants nicely.

1 Cutting the Sections. From a 48x96-inch sheet of ¾-inch plywood, rip three 96-inch-long pieces by 14 inches. Cut the two side sections 80 inches long. Cut the shelves to be 12 inches wide. The bottom toe kick should be 12 inches wide by 4 inches high.

2 Assembling the Sections. Using clamps and glue, fasten the sections together so that all shelves and sides have flush edges. Before you leave the unit to dry overnight, check to see that it's square either by using a carpenter's square or by measuring the diagonals. If you use the diagonal method, adjust the unit until both diagonals are equal.

When the glue is dry, use matching hardwood heat-activated veneer tape to cover the plies of the plywood; then finish the unit with stain or paint, and install it.

Note: This shelf unit can be free-standing; however, it's best to anchor the unit to a wall using small "L" brackets screwed into studs. This way, if someone were to tug on the unit, it wouldn't fall over. Shelves like these also work great as modular units that you can fasten to one another through the end panels using 1¼-inch screws.

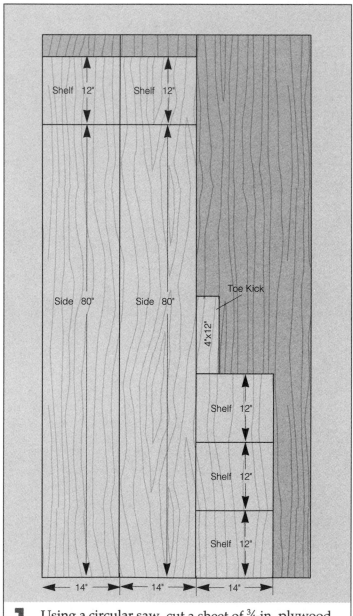

1 Using a circular saw, cut a sheet of ¾-in. plywood according to the diagram. Remember to allow for the saw blade's width when laying out the cut lines.

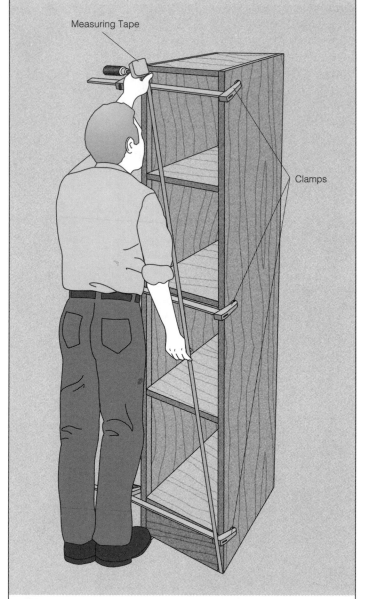

2 Put the glued top shelf in position and clamp it lightly, then the bottom. Continue inserting shelves and clamping, then square and nail up the unit.

Cedar Linings

It's not unusual for the larvae of certain moths to feed on stored clothing and fabric made of natural fibers like wool, as well as on furs. Adding cedar to a closet can keep this type of damage from occurring. Cedar is a species of wood that acts as an effective natural moth repellent, preventing infestation of moth larvae. Cedar also has a pleasant aromatic fragrance and an appealing reddish hue, so it can dress up a drab closet.

The following procedure explains diagonal application of tongue-and-groove cedar planks. The planks can also be installed vertically or horizontally. You can buy packaged cedar planks at many home centers, or purchase the lumber in bulk from a lumberyard. The best walls on which to apply cedar paneling are the ones directly behind hanging clothing and those behind shelves holding sweaters and the like.

Installing Cedar Planks

First, locate and mark the studs. Use a stud finder or, since you'll be covering the walls anyway, probe with a scratch awl until you hit a stud, then measure along the wall at 16-inch intervals to mark the studs. You'll apply the tongue-and-groove cedar boards to the wall with construction adhesive and 6d finishing nails. Squeeze silver-dollar-size dollops of adhesive from a caulking gun onto the backs of the planks every few inches. Then blind-nail the planks by driving nails at a 45-degree angle into the tongue portion of the board. Try to nail into studs wherever possible, but don't worry about it too much because the construction adhesive does a good job of holding the planks to the wall.

Cut the first plank into a right triangle that fits in a bottom corner. Cut the 45-degree angles with a backsaw and miter box or a power miter saw. Face-nail this piece to the bottom plate of the wall. Predrill the nailholes so you don't split the piece. From this corner, work up and outward. When

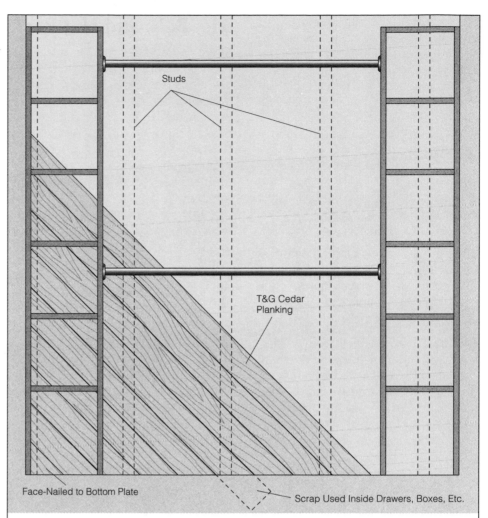

Studs

T&G Cedar Planking

Face-Nailed to Bottom Plate

Scrap Used Inside Drawers, Boxes, Etc.

Cedar Linings. Install cedar behind clothes rods and shelving to protect clothing from damage by moth larvae.

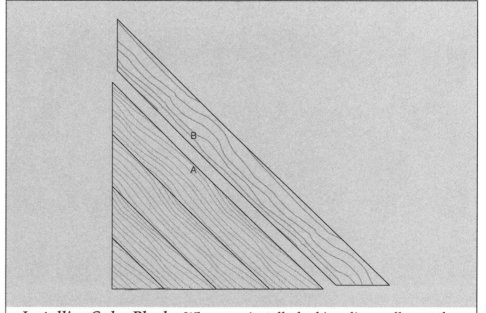

B

A

Installing Cedar Planks. When you install planking diagonally, cut the ends at 45-degree angles, and cut side B ⅛ to ³⁄₁₆ in. longer than side A for a proper fit.

you look at the installation diagram, you might think the longer side of the shorter pieces is equal to the shorter side of the adjacent longer pieces. But as you install the boards along the wall, note that you must make the shorter side of the longer planks about ⅛ to ³⁄₁₆ inch longer than the longer side of the shorter pieces you just installed to make them fit properly. As you approach the end of the wall or section of wall, the pieces you install will become progressively shorter rather than longer.

Wipe the wall down with a dampened rag before rehanging clothes. Never apply a sealer or polyurethane to the paneling; it will hinder the cedar's insect-repelling properties.

Note: To protect clothing stored in drawers, trunks, bags, and boxes, drop in several of the scrap triangles cut from the wall application described above. Before placing these scraps in a storage container, sand all rough edges and wipe the pieces down with a damp rag.

Tie, Belt, and Hat Rack

The doweled hook rack is an attractive and useful storage item that can be used for hanging many things, including ties, belts, hats, mugs, and towels. You can build a simple rack using premilled decorative hardwood dowels, which are commonly available at home centers, craft stores, and woodworking-supply catalogs, and a narrow (3- to 5-inch) strip of matching solid wood or plywood. The dowels come in a variety of styles and in lengths from 1 to 3½ inches.

1 Laying Out and Drilling the Dowel Holes. Depending on its use, determine the spacing between dowels. For a tie or belt rack, set small dowels 1 to 1½ inches on center. For towels and mugs install mid-size dowels 3 inches on center and 3½ inches on center, respectively. For a hat rack, space large dowels on 5- to 6-inch centers. For any of the racks, use either a straight-line pattern or a staggered pattern. Mark the face accordingly.

Using a drill bit that corresponds with the dowel diameter, drill holes into the hardwood or plywood base to a depth slightly past that of the dowel end. If you're drilling with a hand-held power drill, take great care to drill perpendicular to the surface.

2 Installing the Dowels and Finishing the Rack. Smear the dowel ends with wood glue and twist them into the drilled holes. If the dowels seem loose, add a bit of wood dust to the glue smear.

Paint or stain and finish the rack to your preference and allow it to dry. Hang the unit using at least 2-inch wood screws screwed into wall studs or flare-type mollies hammered into a hollow wall space. Drive one screw into each stud that the rack spans or use at least two screws in a hollow wall.

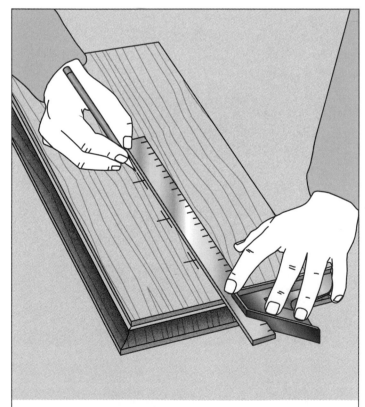

1 Mark the drill holes using a combination square. Space the holes in accordance with what you'll hang from the dowels.

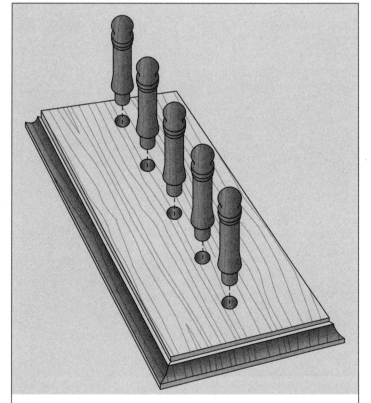

2 Apply glue to the ends of the dowels and into the drilled holes, then insert the dowels into the holes with a slight twist.

BEDROOM STORAGE

Bedrooms are seldom exploited for storage much beyond the bedroom closet. But you can create lots of storage possibilities—under the bed, under windows, in corners—by using some easily obtainable materials and a few tools.

Under-Bed Drawer

In the search for storage opportunities around the house, most of us overlook an area with excellent potential: the space under the bed. Inevitably people put things under the bed anyway. This project provides under-bed storage that's out of sight but readily accessible. This pull-out drawer is just the place for storing off-season clothing, children's toys, or other items. It has an easy-to-open top that keeps stored items dust-free. And you'll never have to struggle to pull the unit in and out because four wooden wheels are installed near the drawer's bottom corners. The wheels are available at most hobby and craft shops or through mail-order suppliers.

Before you begin cutting parts to size, measure the clearance under your bed. The dimensions in the materials list will yield a drawer that measures 6¼ inches high—a size that will fit under most beds. But you can adjust the height of the drawer's sides and ends if your under-bed clearance allows a deeper drawer or demands a shallower one.

Making the Parts

1 **Cutting the Main Parts.** Using ¾-inch plywood, cut two 5¼ x 24-inch sides and two 5¼ x 23¼-inch

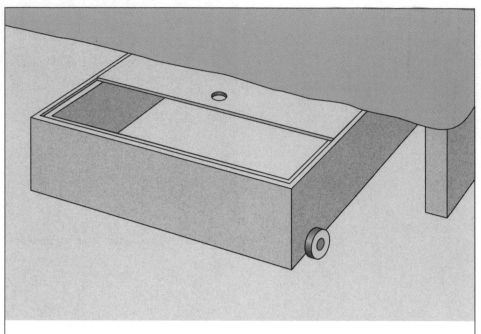

Under-Bed Drawer. A sliding drawer or two with a removable top makes use of ordinarily wasted space under the bed.

panels for the front and back. Also, cut the bottom panel to 23¼ inches square from ⅜-inch plywood and the top panel to 22¾ inches square from ¼-inch plywood.

2 **Cutting the Rabbets.** Rabbet the bottoms and ends of the side panels and the bottoms of the front and back panels. (See page 22 for instructions on how to make a rabbet.) Make the bottom rabbets ⅜ x ⅜ inch and the end rabbets ¾ x ⅜ inch.

3 **Making the Top Edging.** Cut one-by clear pine 2⅛ inches wide and 50 inches long. Cut a 1⅛ x ¼-inch groove down the center of the edging blank. (See page 21 for instructions on how to make a groove.) With a router and ⅜- or ½-inch roundover bit, round-over two corners of the blank as shown. Then rip the blank in half to form two strips of top edging, one to be cut in half for the sides and the other to be cut in half for the front and back.

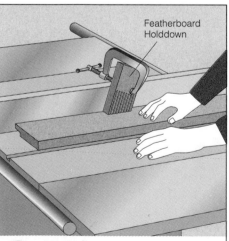

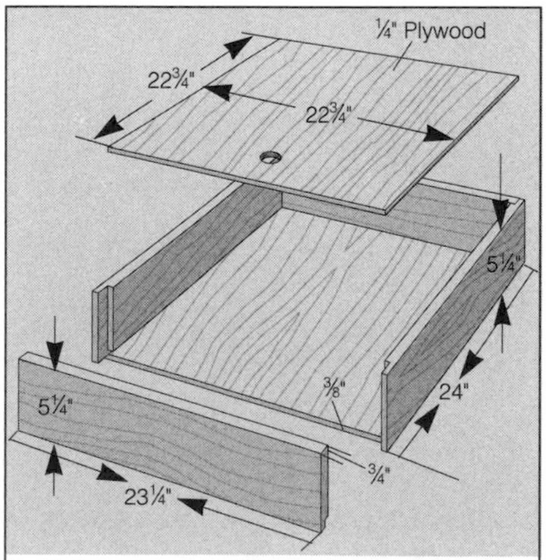

1 Cut the sides, front, and back from ¾-in. plywood. Use ⅜-in. plywood for the bottom and ¼-in. plywood for the top.

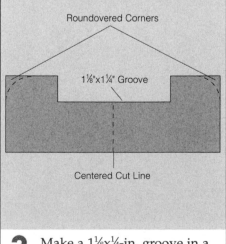

2 Cut ⅜x⅜-in. rabbets in the bottom of the sides, front, and back, and ¾x⅜-in. rabbets in the ends of the side panels

3 Make a 1⅛x¼-in. groove in a 2⅛x50-in. piece of one-by pine. Round-over the edges, then rip the piece in half.

Assembling the Drawer

1 Assembling the Box. Fasten the front and back to the end rabbets in the sides with glue and 6d finishing nails. Fasten the bottom to the bottom rabbets in the box with glue and 1-inch brads. Using a wood knob, center the screw hole for the knob in one end panel and screw the knob in place.

2 Installing the Top Edging. Use a miter box and backsaw or suitable power saw to miter-cut four strips of edging to fit the top edges of the drawer with the rabbets in each strip facing the inside of the drawer. Attach the strips with glue and 4d fin-

ishing nails so that the outside surfaces of the edging and drawer panels are flush. With a 1-inch spade or Forstner bit, drill a finger hole centered about 2 inches from one edge of the plywood top and put the top in place. Paint or stain the drawer assembly after sanding.

3 Installing the Wheels. Obtain 2- to 4-inch wooden wheels with axles, and paint or stain them before installation. Drill two axle holes in each side panel 2 inches inside each front and rear corner and at a distance from the bottom edge to provide ¼-inch clearance when wheels are attached. Insert an axle through each wheel hub, and

glue each axle into a hole, being careful to keep glue off the axle where it contacts the wheel.

Storage Chest-Seat

A chest at the end of a bed is a perfect place to store various bed accessories like extra blankets, pillow cases, and other assorted linens. The closed chest also provides a seat on which to dress and undress. The chest-seat is easy to build because it uses simple rabbet and miter joints.

The chest stands 22 inches high and 18 inches deep. Its width may vary depending on the bed size. Chests that accompany twin beds should be 39 inches wide; those intended for

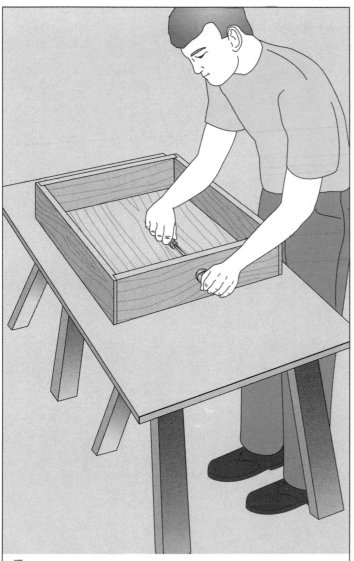

1 Assemble the drawer box on a work table, center a mounting hole in the front panel, and install a wood knob in the hole.

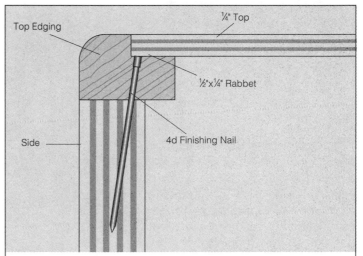

2 Miter-cut four strips of top edging to size and install them on top of the box with 4d finishing nails.

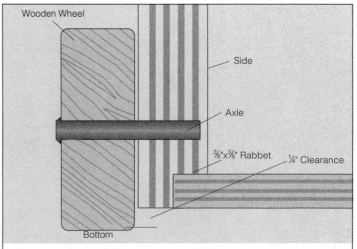

3 Drill two holes in each side for four wooden wheels with axles. Position the holes to provide a ¼-in. clearance for the wheels from the bottom.

double, queen, and king beds should be 54 inches, 60 inches, and 76 inches, respectively. The following procedures describe how to make a chest that will fit a twin bed.

The unit consists of six ¾-inch hardwood plywood slabs—the front and rear panels, two sides, the bottom, and the seat—and common molding. The only hardware the chest requires is a ¾-inch piano hinge the length of the unit and an optional lid-support hinge.

Building the Chest

1 **Cutting the Panels.** Using a table saw or circular saw equipped with a straight-cutting jig, cut the front and back panels and the two side panels from a sheet of plywood. Rip a piece of plywood at a width of 21¼ inches to make the front, rear, and side panels. Crosscut the front and rear sections at 39 inches and the two side sections at 16½ inches.

2 **Cutting the Bottom and Lid.** Cut the bottom section 21¼ x 37½ inches. The grain should run with the longer side. Cut the lid to a width of 19¼ inches by a length of 41½ inches, also with the direction of the grain running with the longer side.

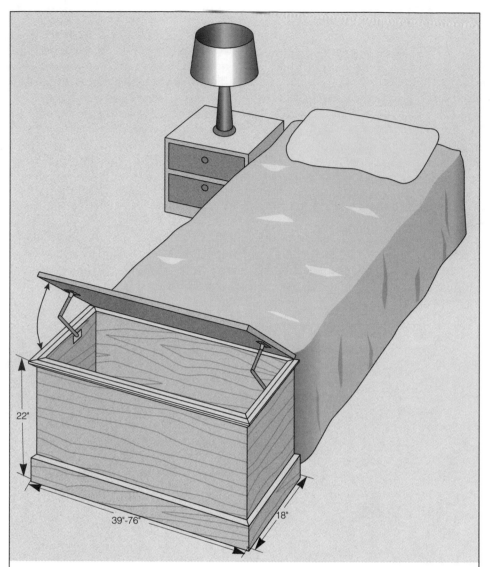

Storage Chest-Seat. Build a combination chest for bedding and seat for dressing from plywood and moldings.

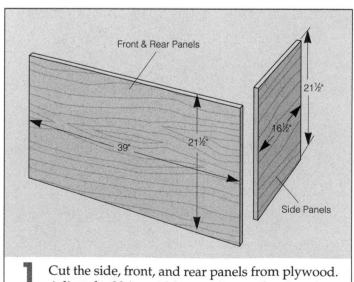

1 Cut the side, front, and rear panels from plywood. Adjust the 39-in. width according to the size of your bed.

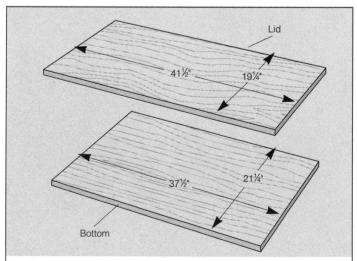

2 From the same kind of plywood you used for the other parts, cut the lid and bottom, with the grain running with the long sides.

3 Veneering the Edges. Using heat-activated veneer tape, veneer the top edges of the front, rear, and side panels, and all four edges of the top lid. These will be the visible edges. At this time also cut four pieces of corner molding 21¼ inches long. You'll trim it later, depending on the height of the base molding you'll use.

4 Cutting and Attaching the Cleats. Rip 3½-inch strips from scrap ¾-inch hardwood plywood. These strips will act as cleats to which the bottom of the chest will be fastened. Altogether there will be four cleats, one each for the front, rear, and two side panels. Cut the side cleats 15 inches long and the front and rear cleats each a total of 37½ inches long. The cleats can be made from single pieces, or you can make them up from several smaller pieces if you don't have scrap that's long enough.

Fasten the cleats to the bottom of the front, rear, and sides using 1¼-inch-long screws in an alternating pattern. Set the cleats flush with the bottom of each panel and with a ¾-inch space at each end.

5 Assembling the Box. Using glue, clamps, and 8d finishing nails, assemble the panels so that the two sides are situated between the front and rear sections. Glue every surface that will mate with another surface to ensure good bond continuity. Face-nail through the front and rear panels into the side panels. Position the nails about ⅜ inch in from the edge of the long panels so they'll be centered on the ¾-inch stock into which you're nailing.

Squeeze glue onto the top of the four cleats while the carcase is still under clamp pressure, then place the bottom section into the box, pushing it and tapping it with the handle end of a hammer until it comes to rest on the top of the cleats. The bottom section will make the box square; however, check that the top corners are square as well with a carpenter's square. With the bottom in place and the unit square and still clamped, allow it to dry overnight.

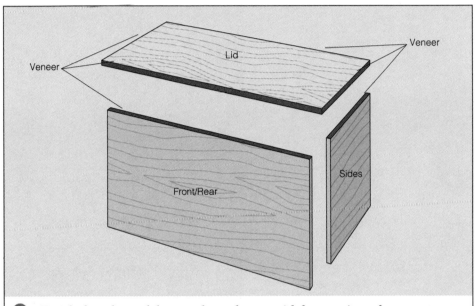

3 Finish the edges of the panels as shown with heat-activated veneer tape. These will be the visible edges.

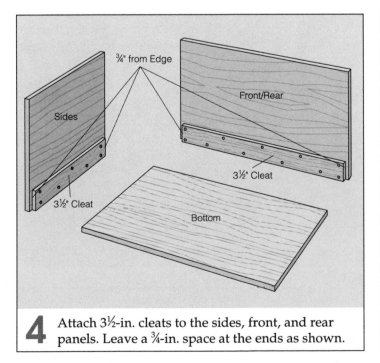

4 Attach 3½-in. cleats to the sides, front, and rear panels. Leave a ¾-in. space at the ends as shown.

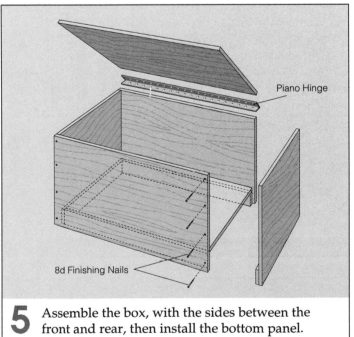

5 Assemble the box, with the sides between the front and rear, then install the bottom panel.

6 Attaching the Moldings.

Around the entire bottom of the assembled chest, wrap a decorative base molding of your choice. The bottom base molding should be about 4 inches high. Miter the corners, then glue and nail the molding with 6d finishing nails. Mark where the bottom edge of the ¾-inch crown molding will fall, then measure, trim, and install the corner molding on all four corners up to the crown molding mark.

Place the crown molding around the top rim of the chest on the front and two sides. Don't nail crown molding to the rear because this would encumber the lid's movement as it opens and closes.

To make nailing easier, lay the chest on its side and place a 2x4 cut to a length of 16½ inches inside the chest so that it spans the middle of the unit. The temporary 2x4 support will firm up your nailing surface: Nailing into a long section of unsupported plywood can be awkward and bouncy.

7 Attaching the Piano Hinge and Lid Support.

Cut and fasten the piano hinge to the top lid using ⅝-inch screws. There are a lot of screws in a piano hinge, so use a battery-powered drill/driver, if you have one, to drive the screws. Leave the pivot end of the piano hinge slightly past the edge of the lid. Then fasten the hinge and lid to the top rear rim of the chest. The piano hinge should extend slightly beyond the rear.

Lid-support hinges (available in hardware stores and woodworkers' supply catalogs) control the opening and closing of the lid and allow it to stay open in any position. This piece of hardware is optional, but it makes using the chest much easier. Fasten one leg of the support hinge to the lid and the other to the inside of one of the side panels. Check the range of motion before you tighten all the screws.

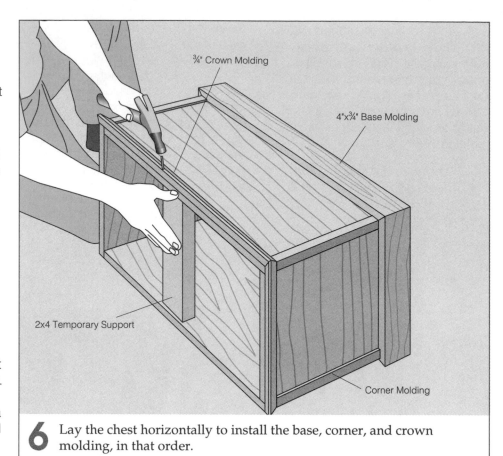

¾" Crown Molding

4"x¾" Base Molding

2x4 Temporary Support

Corner Molding

6 Lay the chest horizontally to install the base, corner, and crown molding, in that order.

7 Attach the piano hinge, first to the lid then to the back panel. You can also install lid-support hinges to hold the lid open in any position.

Soft Netting Corner Shelves

Children's bedrooms are famous for their disorder. Kids accumulate so many things that add to the clutter of their rooms. The trick here is to use air space, the space above the furniture. A tightly bound fisherman's net hung from a corner of a bedroom makes a great place to store soft items like balls, stuffed animals, dolls and pillows. Such "soft shelves" are quite simple to create.

Purchase a fish net with ¼-inch bound loops from a bait and tackle shop. You can also purchase netting in some craft shops, which may come in a variety of colors.

1 **Attaching the Hooks.** Locate the wall studs with a stud finder. Turn ½-inch cup hooks into the wall; start at the corner and be sure to grab a stud. Working out from each side of the corner, place another hook on each wall, equidistant from the first hook. Keep in mind that the diagonal of the net (folded in half) is how far the net "shelf" will extend. If you plan 48 inches or farther from the corner to the end, screw an additional hook to a stud in between.

2 **Hanging the Net.** Fold the net into a triangle, and hang the folded net at the center point from the hook located in the corner. Hang the two corresponding points of the triangle from the farthest hooks out from the corner. Loop the net over any hooks in between as well. Once the net is hung, secure it to the hooks with string so that it can't be pulled off easily, and fill it with soft, lightweight toys.

Window Seat with Drawers

A window seat is a warm, cozy addition to any room. It's equally suitable in a den as an inviting break in a wall full of floor-to-ceiling bookcases as it is in a bedroom. This handsome window seat is designed for double duty with

Soft Netting Corner Shelves. Hang netting across a corner in a child's room to hold stuffed animals and other lightweight toys.

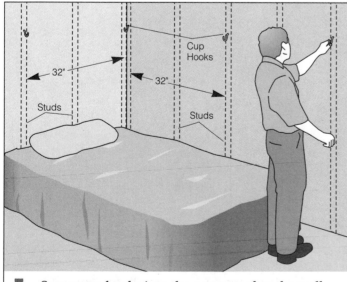

1 Screw cup hooks into the corner and to the wall studs, no farther than 32 in. apart.

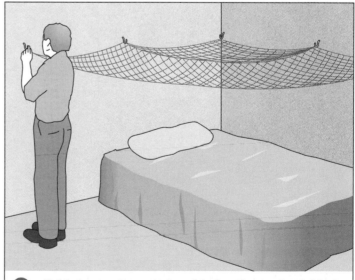

2 Fold the net into a triangle, then hang the folded net from the hooks.

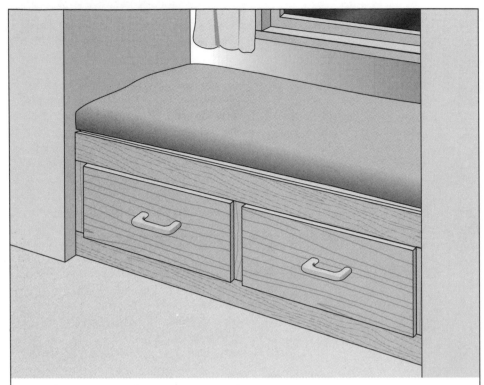

Window Seat with Drawers. Make the area under a window in a bedroom or den do double duty by making a window seat with storage capability.

its comfortable cushions and spacious drawers. As shown, the unit fits a space 48 inches wide, but you can alter the dimensions to fit any available space.

If you have upholstering experience, or if you simply enjoy the challenge,

you can try making your own cushions. Otherwise, have them custommade at a local upholstery shop.

1 Assembling the Face Frame.
Cut two 48-inch-long rails from clear 1x4 stock and three 9¾-inchlong stiles from clear 1x2 stock.

Make a ¾ x ¼-inch rabbet in the top rear edge of the top rail. (See page 22 for how to make a rabbet.)

Use a doweling jig and electric drill to make two holes in each end of each stile. Drill corresponding holes in the center and at both ends of each rail, as shown.

Attach the rails to the stiles with 12 glued dowels. Draw the rails to the stiles with three bar clamps or pipe clamps. Make sure the frame is square and make any necessary adjustments before the glue sets.

2 Cutting and Attaching the Carcase Panels. Cut the back, two sides, and top from ¾-inch plywood. If you build the seat into an alcove, as shown, you can use pine plywood for these pieces. If the unit will be freestanding, you may want to use hardwood plywood. Cut the two sides 16 x 18½ inches, the back 16 x 48 in., and the top 19½ x 48 inches.

Place the back panel against the wall beneath the window, and secure it to the studs with 3-inch screws. Attach the side panels the same way if you are securing them to another wall. If you are securing the side panels to another cabinet, use 1½-inch screws instead.

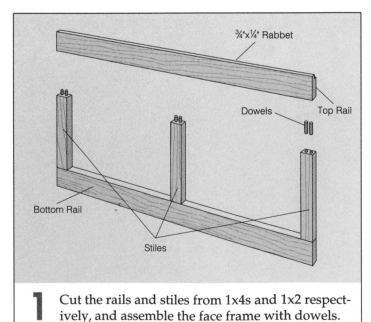

1 Cut the rails and stiles from 1x4s and 1x2 respectively, and assemble the face frame with dowels.

2 Cut the sides, back, and top from plywood, and secure to the back and sides to wall studs.

3 **Installing the Face Frame and Drawer Slides.** Apply glue to the front edges of the side panels, and press the face frame against the glued sides. Secure the frame with four 4d finishing nails, two in each side.

You need to purchase two sets of bottom-mounted roller-bearing drawer slides. At the same time, buy drawer pulls for the drawers. Attach the cabinet portions of the drawer slides to the bottom rail and back panel according to the manufacturer's directions.

4 **Attaching the Top Panel.** Apply glue to the top edges of the carcase and the rabbet in the top of the face frame. Lay the top panel in place, and secure it with 4d finishing nails.

5 **Cutting and Building the Drawers.** Using ¾-inch hardwood plywood, cut the following drawer parts: four sides at 8¾ x 18 inches; two backs at 8⅛ x 20¾ inches; and two fronts at 8¾ x 20¾ inches. Use ⅜-inch plywood to make two drawer bottoms at 17½ x 20¾ inches. The false fronts of the

drawers are solid wood and can be made from clear 1x12 stock. They are larger than the drawer to allow a ⅜-inch overhang on all sides: Cut them 10½ x 22½ inches.

Make ¼x¾-inch rabbets on the inside back and front edges of each of the four sides to accept the front and rear panels as shown in the drawing. To cut the ⅜x¼-inch grooves for the bottoms in the sides and fronts, set the table-saw blade ¼ inch above the table and the rip fence ½ inch away from the blade. This will give the bottom ½-inch clearance for

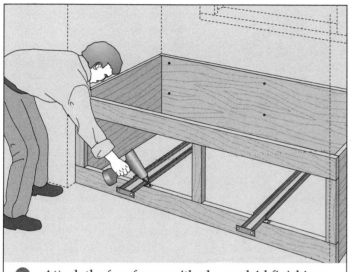

3 Attach the face frame with glue and 4d finishing nails, then fasten bottom-mounted drawer guides.

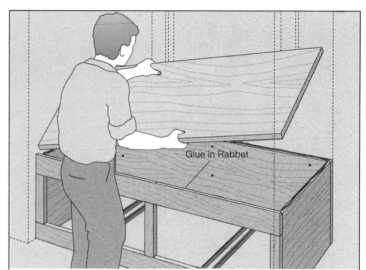

Glue in Rabbet

4 Apply glue to the perimeter of the box, then install the top panel with 4d finishing nails.

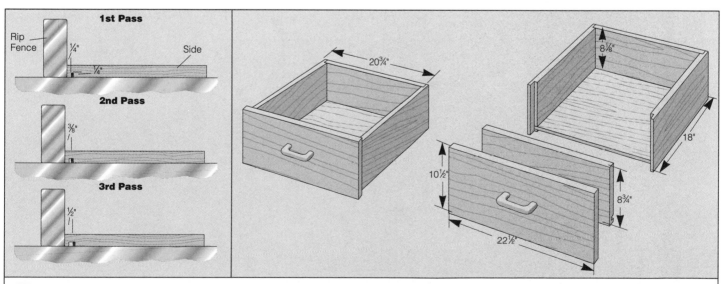

5 Cut the drawer parts—four sides, two backs, two fronts, two bottoms, and two false fronts—to size. Rabbet the edges of the two side pieces, then groove the bottom of the sides, fronts, and backs on the table saw.

the bottom-mounted drawer slides. Run the front panel and each side over the blade to create a ⅛x¼-inch groove. Move the fence ⅛ inch farther from the blade, and run each piece through again to widen the groove to ¼ inch. Move the fence ⅛ inch yet again, and run the pieces through for a third time to make the ⅜-inch grooves.

Apply glue to the front rabbets in the side panels and the ends of the front panel, and attach the side panels to the front with three 3d finishing nails on each side. Slide the bottom panel into position, all the way forward. Apply glue to the rear rabbets in the side panels and to the ends and bottom edge of the rear panel. Put the rear panel in place, flush with the top of the side panels, and nail on the sides. Make sure the drawer is square, then secure the bottom panel to the rear panels with ¾-inch brads.

Fasten each of the false fronts with four #6 x 1¼-inch wood screws driven through countersunk pilot holes near each front inside corner of the drawer.

Attach the drawer portion of the slides to the drawer bottoms, and attach the drawer pulls with the screws provided. Whether you buy them or make them yourself, you'll need two upholstered foam cushions, each measuring 4x20x24 inches.

PVC Laundry Basket

A frame designed to hold a drawstring mesh laundry bag can help in storing and sorting soiled clothes. Placing such a homemade basket inside your closet reduces the number of trips to the laundry room. When it's time to do the wash, simply draw the string and take the sack to the washing machine.

Making the Basket

Select a laundry bag around which to build the holder. The top of the basket should be two to three inches smaller than your chosen mesh bag. You should be able to slip the bag around the top of the

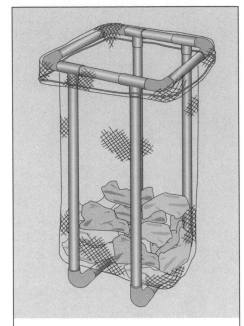

PVC Laundry Basket. A frame made of PVC plumbing pipes and holding a laundry bag, makes a good hamper for use in a closet.

laundry basket and tighten the drawstring under the top tubing. In this fashion, the bag will hang like an open container until you release the drawstring. Use 1¼- or 1½-inch Schedule 20 polyvinyl chloride (PVC) tubing and corresponding fittings to build the frame.

To make the unit illustrated here, you'll need the following:

- ■ Two 10-foot lengths of 1½- or 1¼-inch PVC tubing.

- ■ Four 90-degree PVC street elbows (sized to tubing).

- ■ Four 90-degree PVC regular elbows (sized to tubing).

- ■ Four PVC T-fittings (sized to tubing).

- ■ A small can of clear PVC primer/cleaner.

- ■ A small can of clear PVC adhesive.

- ■ A 32x24-inch laundry bag.

Assembly. Cut sections of tubing with an ordinary handsaw, and test-fit the entire basket. If you're making the frame to fit a laundry bag sized differently from that shown, make the width and depth each one-half the width of the bag, minus ½ inch. Make the height of the frame about 2 inches less than the height of the bag.

If you wish to keep the entire unit portable, you can leave the components unglued. For a stronger hold, however, prime the inside of the fittings and outside of the tubing or the male ends of the street elbows, then apply clear PVC adhesive to both ends and slip the male side into the female side. Hold the parts together for about 20 seconds. When you're finished, clean the entire configuration with the clear PVC cleaner/primer, if necessary. You can then paint the unit with latex acrylic paint if you wish.

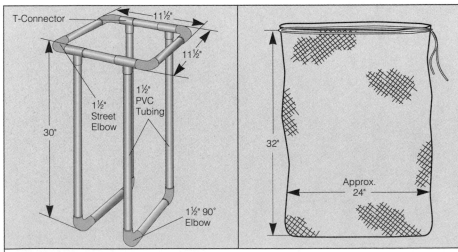

Assembly. Put the frame together using T-connectors, 90-degree street elbows, regular 90-degree elbows, and 1½-in. pipe.

LIVING ROOM, DEN, STUDY, LIBRARY

There are many items to organize in the living room, family room, study, and library, ranging from books and magazines to sleek music CDs and soft, billowing blankets and quilts. The suggestions in this chapter will help you put many of these things in order.

Storage for CDs, Videotapes & Audio Cassettes. The shelf unit shown is designed to hold CDs, but you can size it to hold other media. Bookshelf-style storage (left) is more convenient and adaptable than a slotted arrangement (right).

Storage for CDs, Videotapes & Audio Cassettes

These days, with the ever-increasing popularity of video-cassette recorders (VCRs) and stereo systems that play both music and the soundtracks from movies on VCRs, recorded entertainment cartridges (videotapes, CDs, and audio cassette tapes) are perhaps the most common items stored in the family and/or living room. The basic construction of storage units for these products is similar; only the shelf height and depth vary.

There are many styles of manufactured CD and cassette-tape organizers, both audio and video. Among them all, however, the traditional bookshelf style is most efficient in terms of storage and accessibility. Placing these entertainment cartridges alongside one another like books on a library shelf offers advantages over other storage-system styles:

■ Most people arrange their collections in some type of order, whether it's alphabetical by artist or by musical category or both. Adding a new cartridge to such a collection is easy in a bookshelf-like system: Just slide the

rest of the collection one way or the other. Other systems, such as the "slotted" type, require moving almost the entire collection each time you add one CD or tape.

■ Double cassettes pose no problem because there are no slots of a predetermined size.

Building the Unit

This project describes how to build a CD storage unit, but with only slight alterations to shelf size and height, you can modify the design to make a videotape or audiotape holder. Note that the back of the case is made of ¾-inch plywood. It is the back that is most important to the unit's structural integrity since it holds the whole case together and is the mounting point for the unit on the wall.

1 Cutting the Parts. Cut all the sections for the shelf unit from ¾-inch plywood. The overall unit size is up to you, but the usable space on the shelves should be no more than 30 inches in width. Shelves with wider spans can sag over time.

Cut the rear panel first. A four-shelf CD unit, which has a back that measures 30 inches wide by 24¼ inches high, is illustrated in the drawings. A one-shelf unit's rear panel will be

5½ inches high, with each shelf height adding 6¼ inches.

Cut the shelves 30½ inches wide and 5¾ inches deep. The shelves will fit into ¼-inch-deep dadoes in each side section. The side, top, and bottom sections should be ¾-inch deeper than the corresponding shelves, or in this case, 6½ inches deep. This will accommodate the ¾-inch rear section over which the sides, top, and bottom overlap. Cut the top and bottom 30½ inches wide; cut the sides 25¾ inches high, or 1½ inches longer than the height of the rear section.

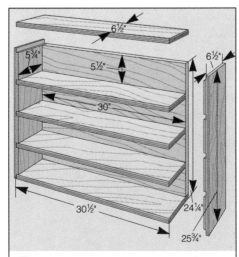

1 Cut the parts for the shelf unit from ¾-in. plywood, making it no more than about 30 in. wide.

2 Cutting the Dadoes. Position and mark the three shelves with at least 5½ inches between them. You'll cut ¾-inch dadoes and rabbets ⅜ inch deep. Clamp the two side sections alongside one another to plow the dadoes and rabbets. This will ensure that the dadoes of both side sections correspond with one another.

3 Assembling the Unit. Assemble the unit using glue, bar clamps, and 6d finishing nails as shown in the drawing. Fasten the top and bottom to the side sections first, then set the rear panel into place. From a side view there should be no visible top or bottom edges. Face-nail the sections together with the nails. Always use glue along with nailing.

Using a carpenter's square, position the shelves and nail them in place as well. Make sure the shelves are square with the rear section. Allow the assembly to dry overnight before handling it.

4 Veneering the Front Edges. Using 30 to 50 feet of heat-activated veneer tape (according to the size of your unit), veneer all the front edges. Sand and finish the unit accordingly.

5 Hanging the Unit. Hang the unit at eye level so that CDs (or video or audio cassettes) can be easily viewed. If your youngsters are allowed to play tapes themselves, you may consider a lower unit dedicated to children's tapes.

Note: One 30-inch-wide shelf holds approximately 75 CDs. Keep in mind the rate at which you'll expand your collection. The unit you build should be large enough to accommodate a few years' growth.

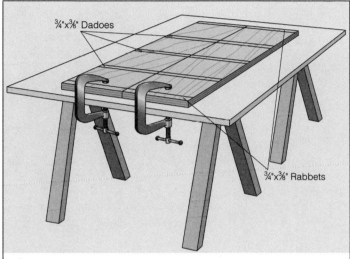
¾"x⅜" Dadoes
¾"x⅜" Rabbets

2 Clamp the sides next to each other on a work surface and cut ¾-in. dadoes at least 5½ in. apart for the shelves.

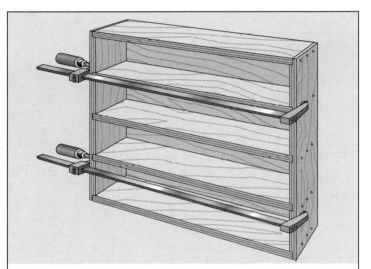

3 Assemble the sides, top, and bottom around the rear panel, then install the shelves, gluing and nailing all the pieces.

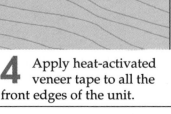

4 Apply heat-activated veneer tape to all the front edges of the unit.

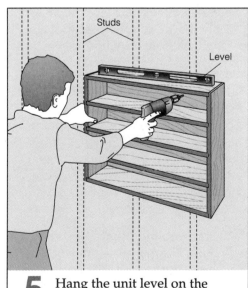
Studs
Level

5 Hang the unit level on the wall and attached to studs at about eye level.

Suggested Shelf Dimensions for Entertainment Media

Entertainment Medium	Shelf Depth	Shelf Height
CD	5¾"	5½"
Audio Tape Cassette	3"	5"
Videotape Cassette	5¾"	9½"

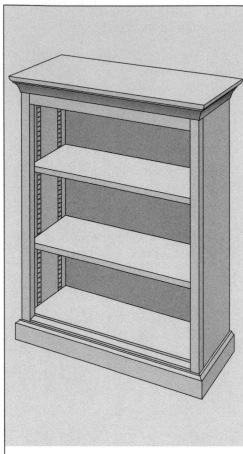

Bookcase. Make a traditional bookcase with adjustable shelves, and you can store books and display pictures and collectibles as well.

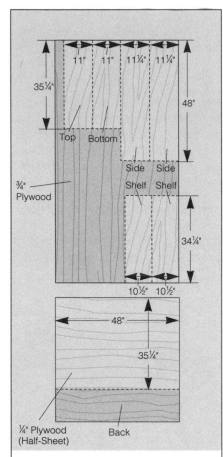

1 Cut the carcase parts from a full sheet of ¾-in. plywood and a half sheet of ¼-in. plywood.

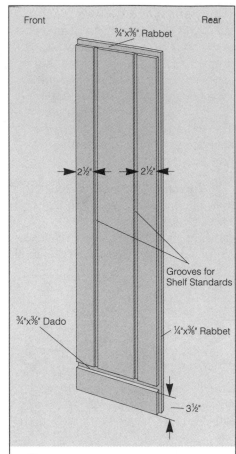

2 Cut rabbets, dadoes, and grooves into both side panels. Make sure the cuts are identical in each panel.

Bookcase

Here's a lovely classical bookcase that you can assemble in less than a day. Although its construction is simple, this bookcase will impress you with its pleasant proportions and versatility. Its compact size and adjustable shelves serve well in a family room, den, or study, or even a bedroom, to display books or showcase your favorite mementos.

The cove and baseboard moldings give the piece a formal appearance, reminiscent of larger, built-in cabinets. The look is further enhanced by the solid hardwood top with a quarter-round edge detail. If you choose, you can make the side panels of hardwood plywood to match the solid-wood top. Or you can emphasize the solid-wood top by painting the case.

1 **Cutting the Main Parts.** Using ¾-inch plywood, cut the two sides 11¼x48 inches, the top and bottom panels 11x35¼ inches each, and the two shelves 10½x34½ inches. Cut the back panel 35¼x48 inches from a half-sheet of ¼-inch plywood.

2 **Cutting the Rabbets and Dadoes.** Rabbet, dado, and groove the side panels as shown. (See pages 21 and 22 for how to make rabbets, dadoes, and grooves.) Note that the drawing shows only one panel. Don't forget to make the other panel as a mirror image.

3 **Assembling the Carcase and Face Frame.** Assemble the top and bottom to the side panels with glue and 4d finishing nails. Install the back panel with glue and 4d finishing nails.

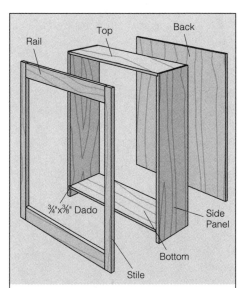

3 Put the top, bottom, sides and back together with glue and 4d finishing nails. Cut the stiles and rails from 1x2s and 1x4s, respectively, and attach them to the carcase with 4d nails.

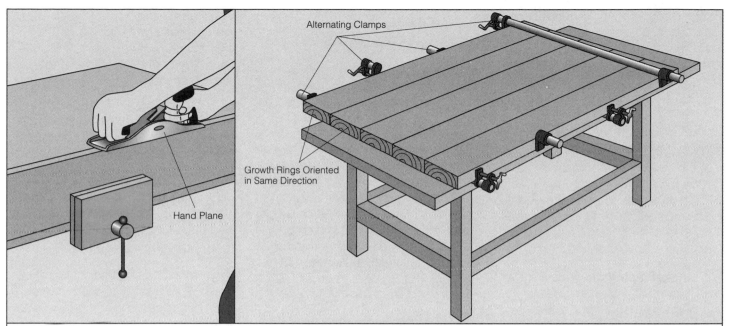

4 Make the top by planing the edges of one-by lumber and gluing them up with alternating clamps as shown. Cut the top to size, sand it smooth, and round-over the edges with a router.

Cut the two stiles to a length of 48 inches from 1x2s and the two rails to a length of 33 inches from 1x4s. Attach the rails and stiles to the carcase with glue and 4d finishing nails. Be sure the top edges of the top and bottom rails are flush with the top and bottom panels, respectively.

4 Making the Solid-Wood Top.
Make the top by edge-gluing several one-by boards and cutting the solid panel to the final dimension of 13½x39 inches. Carefully plane the edges of the one-bys square with a large hand plane. Check the ends of the boards for the direction of the annual growth rings in the wood and orient all the boards in the same direction. Apply glue to all the edges to be glued, and using as many clamps as necessary, clamp the panel together. Make sure you alternate the clamps above and below the panel for even clamping pressure and check that all the boards are aligned, with no edges sticking up. Clean off any glue squeeze-out with a wet rag or by peeling off the excess once it has become rubbery but before it hardens. When the glue has cured, plane or sand the panel smooth and cut it to size.

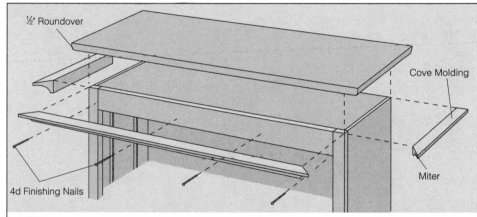

5 Attach the top, rounded side down, and secure cove molding to the perimeter. Miter-cut and attach the base molding.

After sanding the top to 220-grit, decide which surface will be the bottom. Then mark layout lines on the bottom to indicate how the solid-wood top will be positioned on the case. The top should overhang the case by 1½ inches at the front and sides. The top and case should be flush at the back.

Fit a router with a ½-inch roundover bit. Shape the bottom edges of the front and two sides of the solid-wood top, making several progressively deeper passes until the three bottom edges are rounded over ½ inch. Turn over the workpiece, then round the front and side edges with sandpaper.

5 Installing the Top and Molding.
Turn the top upside down and position the case upside down on the top. At each corner, drill for 1¼-inch screws into the top piece. Remove the top. Make the holes in the case oblong by inserting the drill in the holes and rocking from the front of the case to the back. (This will allow the solid wood top to expand and contract with humidity changes.) Then counterbore the holes. Replace the top and screw it in place.

Cut a piece of ⅞-inch cove molding for the front to rough length (finished length: 37½ inches), mitered at one end. Test its fit beneath the overhanging top, mark the squared end, miter-cut it to finished length, and install it with 4d finishing nails. Miter-cut one end of each side piece of cove to rough length (finished length: 12¾ inches). Set each side piece in place, mark the rear of each, cut it to finished length, and install it with glue and 4d finishing nails.

Cut a piece of 2½-inch base molding for the front to its finished length of 37½ inches, mitered at each end. Glue and nail it along the front edge. Test fit and install the side pieces as you did the cove molding.

6 **Installing the Shelves.** Cut two pieces of ⅜x¾-inch half-round molding to the length of the shelves you cut in Step 1. Attach the molding to the shelves with glue and 1-inch brads.

Use a hacksaw to cut the shelf standards to fit between the top and bottom panels, and install the standards inside the grooves in the bookcase sides, using the screws or nails provided or recommended. Install each shelf with four metal shelf supports.

Hanging Magazine Rack

In the spirit of conserving floor space, a convenient place to store and display magazines is on a wall near your other media collections. Someone selecting a CD from a shelf may want to pick out a magazine to read or flip through while listening to the CD. You can easily build a magazine rack in about two hours using one-by solid wood or ¾-inch plywood. The project requires only basic tools and uses simple butt joints in its assembly.

Building the Rack

Cut the two side sections 12 inches long by 6 inches wide. Make sure the grain follows the long dimension. At one end of each side piece, measure 4 inches across the 6-inch side and make a mark. Using a straightedge, draw a line from the 4-inch mark to the corresponding corner on the other end of each of the boards and cut along the line.

You'll end up with two 12-inch-long side pieces that taper along one side from 6 inches wide to 4 inches wide. If you prefer you can angle the top section.

Cut the rectangular rear section 9x11¼ inches and the bottom section 4x9 inches, both with the grain following the longer dimension. Set the bottom section at a right angle against the 4-inch end of a side piece and scribe the line made by the angled edge of the side piece. Bevel the edge of the bottom to this mark (about a 10-degree bevel).

For the horizontal slats, rip a 1-inch-wide piece from a 10-inch-long one-by. Then slice two ¼-inch-thick slats from the 1-inch face on a table saw.

Using glue, clamps, and 6d finishing nails, assemble the rack so that the two side sections flank the rear and bottom sections as shown in the drawing. If you're using plywood, cover the exposed ends with veneer tape. Tack the front supports using a dab of glue and one 4d finishing nail.

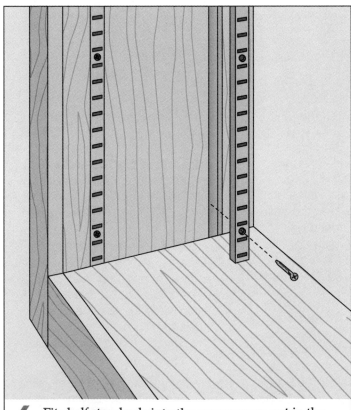

6 Fit shelf standards into the grooves you cut in the side panels to accept the adjustable shelving.

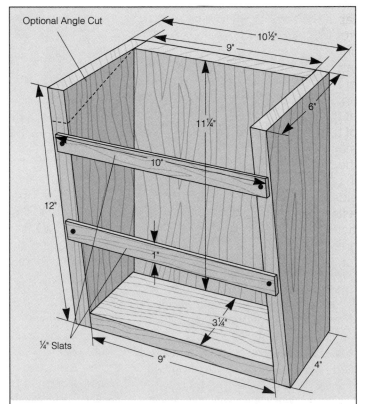

Building the Rack. This magazine rack can be made of ¾-in. plywood or one-by pine or hardwood.

Hanging Quilt Rack

A classic way to store and display decorative quilts is on a rack. Traditionally, quilt racks are freestanding and therefore take up floor space. But you can free up that space by hanging a rack on a wall.

The quilt rack's design borrows the elongate arc from the Craftsman style of architecture. You'll build the rack using a combination of ¾-inch hardwood plywood, solid one-by stock, and three 4-foot, 1¼-inch-diameter rails. The rack assembly has no complicated joints and no hardware. The top of the quilt rack does double duty as additional shelf space for your favorite books, frames, or memorabilia.

Making the Rack

1 Cutting the Sections. Cut the following parts from ¾-inch hardwood plywood: a 42x19½-inch rear section, two 9¾ x 19½-inch sides, and a 9x42-inch top section

With its good side facing up, clamp one of the side sections to a work table. At a point 22½ inches away from the edge of the section and in line with the bottom, tap a finish nail into the work surface. Tie one end of a piece of string around the nail and the other end around a pencil at a distance of 27 inches. The point of the pencil should be approximately 4½ inches from the edge of the side section. Once the pencil is in place, trace an arc through the side section. The arc should leave a flat area of about 4½ inches at the bottom of the side piece, and a flat area of 2¾ inches at the top. Repeat for the other side section, but with the good side face down.

2 Boring the Rail Holes. With a Forstner bit, which creates holes that have a flat bottom, bore three 1¼-inch-diameter, ½-inch-deep stopped holes on the inside surface of each side section. The holes in the two sides should correspond with each other (see the drawing for hole placement). Set a depth of ½ inch on

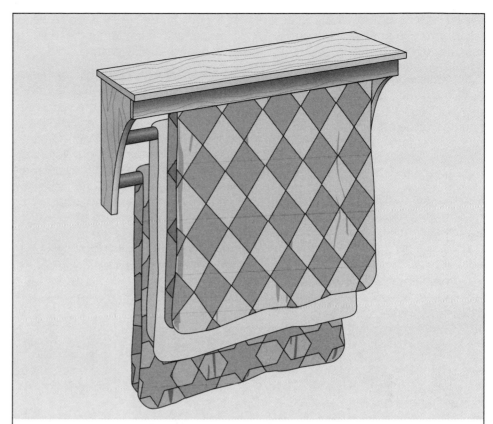

Hanging Quilt Rack. Mount this unusual rack in the family room, and you can hang decorative quilts and display collectibles on the generous shelf space. The rack is made from ¾-in plywood, clad with solid lumber on the top and front.

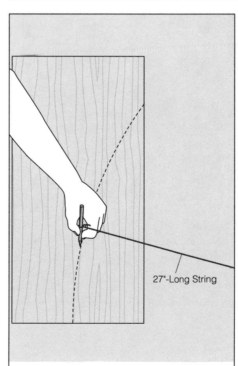

1 Cut the top, side, and rear to size from ¾-in. plywood. Use a 27-in.-long piece of string to make the arc cut lines in the sides.

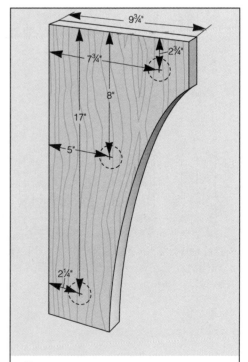

2 Bore 1¼-in.-diameter, ½-in.-deep holes on the inside of each side piece, carefully positioned as shown.

the bit with a piece of masking tape to be sure you don't drill through to the other side.

3 Assembling the Rack.

Cut the 1¼-inch-diameter rails to 42½ inches long, then fit the rails into each side section. Coat the ends of the rails and the inside of the holes with glue, and drive one 8d finishing nail into each rail from the outside.

Lay the rear section on a workbench, face up, then fasten the sides to the rear section using glue and face-nailed 8d finishing nails. The side sections should lap the ends of the

rear section. Be sure the top of the side panel and the top of the rear section are exactly flush.

With the sides fastened, glue and nail the plywood top section in place with 8d finishing nails. Turn the frame around, and fasten the rear section to the rough top section with 1¼-inch screws through predrilled holes. Turn the frame around face-up again and affix the rough front section, which will fit under the top section and between the sides.

4 Assembling the Finished Sections.

Glue up the finish

top close to final size (see page 61 for how to make a solid-wood panel) and finish-cut it to 12x46 inches. Cut the finish face from one-by stock to 3x43½ inches. Glue, clamp, and screw the finish top and face from inside the unit with 1¼-inch screws to avoid marring the visible surfaces. Overhang the top 1¼ inches on each side and 1½ inches at the front. Under the top, miter and fasten 1⅛x¾ crown molding with 4d finishing nails.

Install the unit on a wall, attaching it to studs with 3-inch-long screws through the rear panel just below the top.

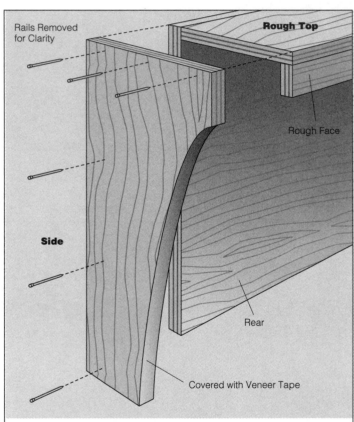

Rails Removed for Clarity

Rough Top

Rough Face

Side

Rear

Covered with Veneer Tape

3
Assemble the rough body parts of the rack with butt joints, glue, and nails. Install the rails before assembling the sides to the rear, top, and face panels, in that order. Use nails for the sides and screws for the rear panel.

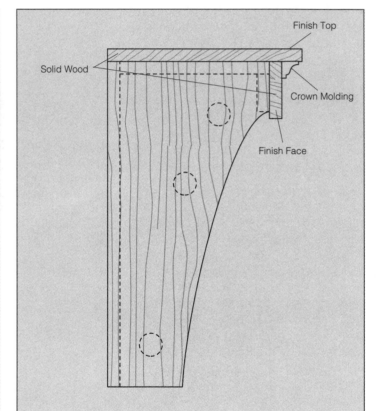

Solid Wood

Finish Top

Crown Molding

Finish Face

4
Glue-up and cut the finish top, then cut the finish face and install them from the inside with 1¼-in. screws. Attach crown molding under the top's overhang, apply finish, then mount the unit to wall studs with 3-in. screws.

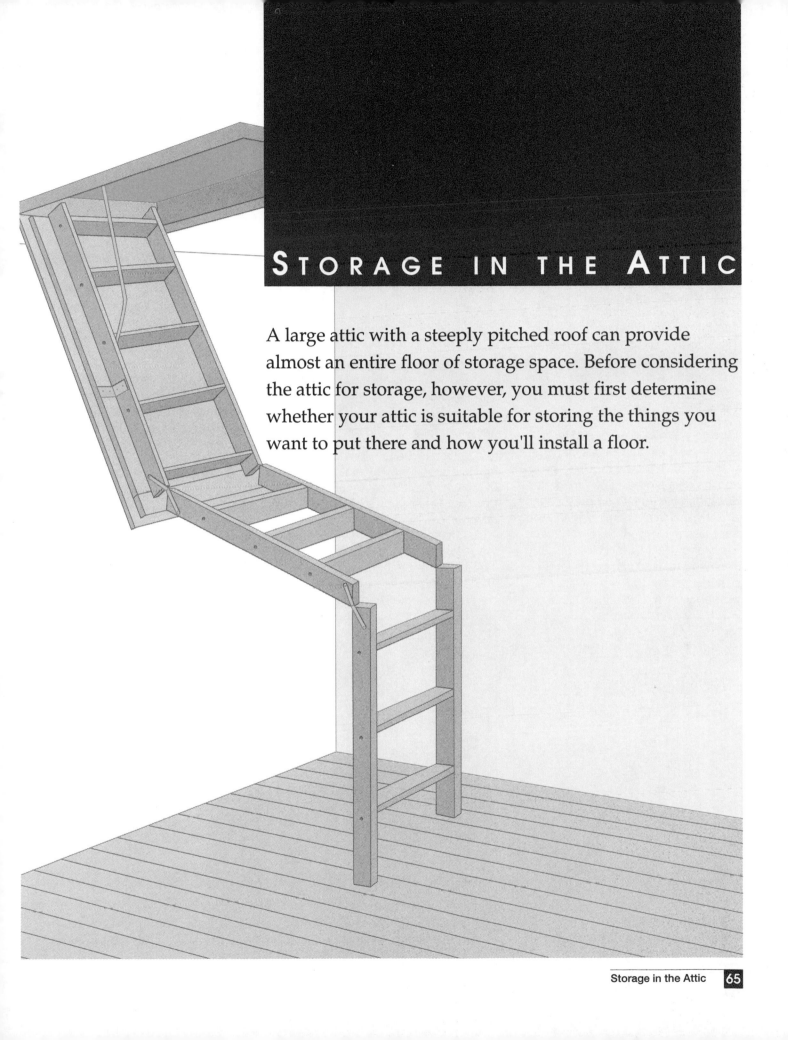

STORAGE IN THE ATTIC

A large attic with a steeply pitched roof can provide almost an entire floor of storage space. Before considering the attic for storage, however, you must first determine whether your attic is suitable for storing the things you want to put there and how you'll install a floor.

Precautions & Considerations

Temperature. In summer, an attic can reach temperatures above 110 degrees Fahrenheit. In winter, a properly insulated attic not being used as living space will be the same temperature as it is outdoors, less the wind chill. Humidity in an attic can also vary greatly, so any items stored in the attic must be able to withstand these varying conditions.

Joist Size. Small joists like 2x4s and 2x6s, such as might be used in truss construction, may not be strong enough to support additional weight. The size and span of a joist determine the amount of load that can be placed on it. Check with an architect or engineer concerning your attic span and joist size.

Flooring. When insulation extends above the tops of the joists in the attic, you may have to add blocking before you install a storage floor in an attic. Adding flooring that compresses the existing insulation results in reduced heat-loss protection. Screw 2x2s on top of the joists as the blocking. If you need to use lumber of a larger dimension than 2x2, your joists are probably not strong enough to sup-port much additional weight. Consult a building engineer.

Recessed Lighting. Never cover recessed lighting that is not thermally protected or clad in a thermal-resistant casing. Check with an architect or building official in your area for rules and procedures for working around recessed lighting.

Nailing. Use screws rather than nails when attaching materials to an attic floor. The percussion from hammering can damage the ceilings below the attic. Screws are significantly less damaging.

Folding Attic Stairway

Folding stairs are intended to provide access to an attic. When you need to get into the attic, you pull down the stairs; when you're done with them, they fold back up into the attic.

Placement of the attic pull-down staircase is important. The stairs must be accessible, and they should disturb as little of the ceiling's existing framing as possible. Because most pull-down units are not energy efficient, it should be placed in an area that can be isolated to minimize heat loss. Lastly, there must be sufficient headroom for someone entering the attic.

Folding stairs are sold as kits at building-supply outlets and are designed to be installed quickly. You may have several styles and sizes to choose from, and installation details may vary among them. The instructions that follow are typical of standard folding-stairway designs, but follow the manufacturer's specific recommendations.

1 Locating the Stairs. Locate the stairs where there's sufficient room to swing the ladder open. There should be room enough— 24 to 36 inches—for a person to walk in front of the extended ladder. Check the dimensions required for installing a folding stairway before you buy one.

Because most disappearing staircases aren't designed for heat loss protection, adding a unit means sacrificing the total insulating value of the attic ceiling. This can be more of a problem if the unit is located in a common hallway that's open to the entire house. Try to locate the unit in a small room that can be isolated by closing a door. Putting the unit in a walk-in closet with a door would be ideal.

2 Framing the Rough Opening. Disappearing staircases vary in size, with a rough opening of from

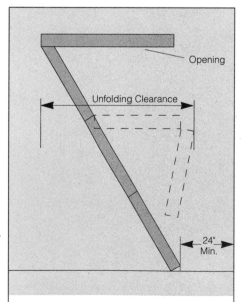

1 Follow the manufacturer's instructions to determine the best location for the stairs.

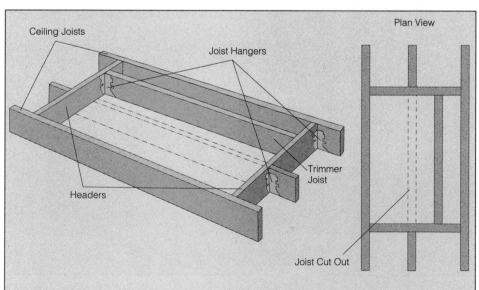

2 Most attic stairs are installed parallel with the ceiling joists. Frame the rough opening by cutting out a section of a joist and installing two headers and one trimmer. Use joist hangers.

22 to 30 inches wide and 48 to 60 inches long. Orient the opening parallel with the existing ceiling joists, disturbing only a minimum of the existing ceiling framing. You'll have to cut a section out of at least one joist, then install headers and trimmers to create the rough opening. Using a stud finder from the floor below, identify where the attic joists are in the ceiling. Mark the joists on the ceiling surface, and use a carpenter's square to trace the outline of the rough opening. Start from an edge of a joist so that the opening spans evenly between the joists, minimizing the number of cuts you'll have to make. Cut out the drywall with a utility knife and/or drywall saw.

With a reciprocating saw, cut the middle joist 1½ inches beyond the ceiling opening at both ends to accommodate the headers you'll place across the opening. The illustration shows the installation of two headers and a trimmer. Use joist hangers to join joists, headers, and trimmers.

3   Installing Temporary Supports. Temporarily screw 1x4 supports across the ends of the rough opening so that they form a 1-inch ledge in the opening. Drive 2-inch drywall screws through the 1x4 supports into the headers on both ends of the rough opening. The supports will be required to carry the full weight of the stairs as you fasten the unit in place.

4   Installing the Stairs. With a helper in the attic, slide the stairway unit up into the rough opening, and rest it on the temporary supports. Make sure you've placed it in the right direction. Level and square the stairs, using wood shims if necessary. Carefully unfold the stairs, then drive 16d finishing nails through the stairway frame into the joists. Trim the bottom of the stairs flush with the floor so that when unfolded, the ladder forms a straight line. Remove the temporary supports, and trim around the opening with casing that matches your home's existing molding.

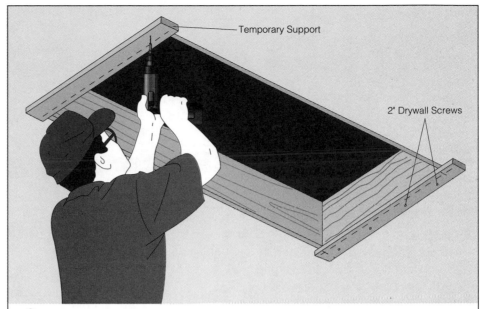

3   Screw 1x4s along each end of the rough opening so that they create a ledge to support the stairs temporarily.

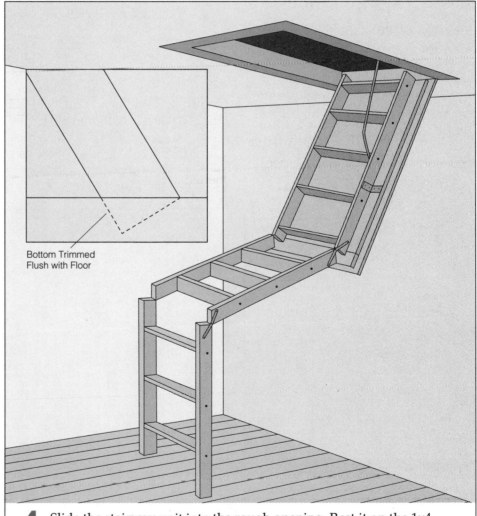

4   Slide the stairway unit into the rough opening. Rest it on the 1x4 supports. When the unit is level and square, secure it with 16d nails. Trim the bottom of the stairs.

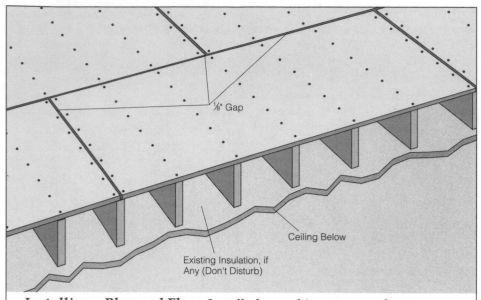

Installing a Plywood Floor. Install plywood in a staggered pattern so you avoid adjacent joints. Don't compress any existing insulation.

Attic Storage Floor

Most attics were designed to support some additional weight. Check with an architect or engineer, however, to see whether your attic will support the loads you're planning to store there.

It's difficult and often dangerous to work in an attic, so create a work area at another location, such as the floor directly below the attic. Make your measurements in the attic but cut the lumber and plywood at your workstation.

Often the small size of an attic hatch, the low headroom of a shallow roof, or a combination of both will restrict your ability to maneuver full sheets of 4x8-foot ¾-inch plywood into the attic. To maneuver through these tight spaces, rip sheets in half lengthwise. Make sure that when you fasten the ripped sheets to the attic joists, you place them side by side in the same configuration they were in before being cut. This arrangement is especially important if you're using a circular saw and chalk line to rip sheets in half, which is a less accurate method than using a table saw.

Installing a Plywood Floor

Always install plywood in a staggered fashion, so that no two full-length sections end on the same joist. Starting with a one-half or one-third sheet of plywood will ensure good placement. Fasten the plywood using 1¼-inch drywall screws instead of traditional flooring nails.

Leave a gap of about 8 to 10 inches where the rafters and joist intersect. Blocking this area with plywood can prevent proper ventilation. The same is true when installing batt insulation. Blocking ventilation paths can result in a host of temperature and humidity problems in your attic and roof.

Attic Drawer Storage

Ordinarily, the most useless space in an attic is the area along the eaves about 4 to 5 feet from the intersection of the roof rafters and attic floor joists. The height of this space is so restrictive that it is

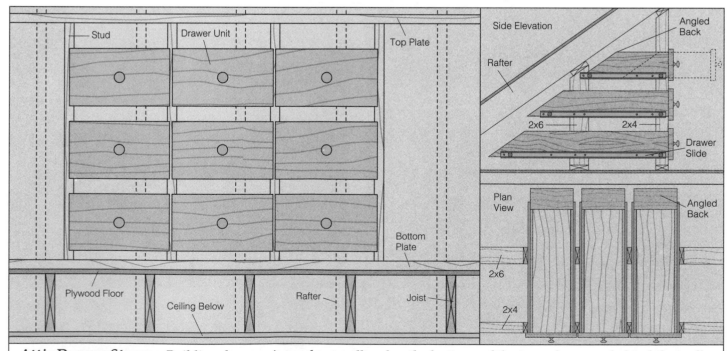

Attic Drawer Storage. Building drawers into a kneewall makes the best use of the irregular space behind the wall.

generally considered dead space. This space can be used, however, by installing drawer units between two small walls called kneewalls.

A kneewall is a wall built from the attic floor to the angled roof rafters above. Using the studs of such kneewalls as drawer frames, you can convert the dead space in your attic into a utility storage drawer unit. You can use one drawer, two drawers, or three as shown. Install one or more banks of drawers according to your storage needs.

1 **Laying an Air Barrier.** Using an air-infiltration barrier, or "house wrap" (sometimes known by the trade names Typar or Tyvek), surround the drawer area. The barrier is permeable to vapor but will protect the drawer contents and the drawer unit itself from water and dust. Do not use a vapor barrier like plastic or polyethylene since these cause "sweating" and could also disturb the overall ventilation of the attic roof.

Staple the barrier along the floor if there's no subfloor and up the rafter ceiling to where the larger kneewall will be. At the top, leave enough barrier wrap to drape in front of the drawer front. Add the barrier wrap to the two sides as well; this will encapsulate the entire unit.

2 **Building the Kneewalls.** The height of the kneewall depends largely on the slope and span of your attic rafters. The top height of the smaller (rear) kneewall, however, should be approximately at the bottom of the top drawer. Frame the smaller kneewall with 2x6s.

Align the 2x6 bottom plate with the house's framing so that it's parallel to the outside walls. Fasten the plate to the floor with wood screws. At both ends of the bottom plate, use a level to make a plumb mark from the front of the bottom plate to the rafters above. Connect one plumb mark to the other by snapping a chalk line across the rafters. These plumb marks will indicate the front face of the studs.

1 Staple house-wrap material to the joists and rafters in the attic where you'll build the kneewall.

Using the top chalk line as a guide, fasten a 2x6 top plate to the rafters. Because the top plate is angled and will not align with the bottom plate if placed directly on the chalk line, offset it from the line so that the underside of the top plate aligns with the outside of the bottom plate, as in the drawing.

To cut the studs for the kneewall, first find the appropriate angle for the top cut on these studs. To find this angle, simply plumb any stud against a rafter and scribe where the rafter intersects the stud. Cut the stud and use it as a template for the others.

The space between the studs is a matter of preference but will determine the width of the drawers: Each bay between two studs supports a bank of drawers. Smaller drawers may not be as useful as larger ones, but make the drawers no wider than 36 inches. Make sure the studs are plumb and perpendicular to the plates.

Frame the taller kneewall following the procedures for the rear wall, but

use 2x4s instead of 2x6s. Make sure the studs of the larger wall are exactly perpendicular to the studs in the smaller wall. Use a carpenter's square to align the studs. Alignment is important since the drawers will glide through both sets of studs, front and rear.

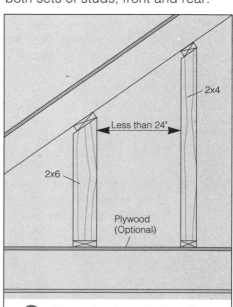

2x4

Less than 24"

2x6

Plywood (Optional)

2 Place the front 2x4 wall studs less than 24 in. from the rear wall.

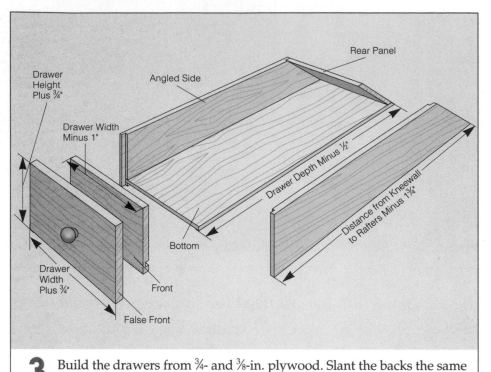

Drawer Height Plus ¾"

Drawer Width Minus 1"

Drawer Width Plus ¾"

Angled Side

Rear Panel

Drawer Depth Minus ½

Distance from Kneewall to Rafters Minus 1¼"

Bottom

Front

False Front

3 Build the drawers from ¾- and ⅜-in. plywood. Slant the backs the same angle as that of the roof slope.

3 Building the Drawers. The drawers are built the same way as those in the window seat (page 55), except that these drawers have a slanted back. For each drawer you'll need ¾-inch plywood for the two sides, the back, and the front. You can use plywood or solid wood for the false front panel, which has a ⅜-inch overlay. Use ⅜-inch plywood for the bottom.

Determine how deep you want the drawers to be and cut the sides and front accordingly. You'll loose ⅝ inch because of the bottom (⅜ inch for the depth of the panel and ¼ inch of clearance below the bottom panel), so take this dimension into account when you figure the drawer depth. Measure the distance from the face of the tall kneewall to within about 1¾ inches of the rafters, and cut the sides to the same angle as the roof rafters. Cut the rear panel to the proper depth and bevel the top and bottom at the same angle as the sides. The back panel rests on top of the bottom panel, so take this into account when you measure. Cut ¼x¾-inch rabbets in the front and back of the two side pieces to

accept the front and back panels. Cut the front, back, and bottom panels to match the distance between the studs, minus 1½ inches (allowing for ½ inch of clearance on each side of the drawer for the slide hardware). Cut the bottom to the same length

as the sides, minus ½ inch. Cut ¼x⅜-inch grooves for the bottom panel in the side and front pieces, ¼ inch up from the bottom edges.

Assemble the front and two sides with glue and 3d finishing nails. Slide the bottom panel into place, then attach the back panel with glue and 3d nails. Attach the bottom panel to the rear with ¾-inch brads. Cut the false front to size, and attach it to the front of the drawer from the inside with 1¼-inch drywall screws.

4 Attaching the Slide Hardware. You need to purchase a pair of side-mounted roller-bearing drawer slides for each drawer. At the same time, buy drawer pulls for the drawers. Attach the drawer portions of the slides to the drawers according to the manufacturer's directions. Attach the wall side sections of the drawer slides to the 2x4 front wall studs and the 2x6 wall studs behind. Put two screws through the drawer slides into the 2x6 studs to keep the slide secure when the drawer extends beyond the small wall into the corner of the rafter-joist intersection.

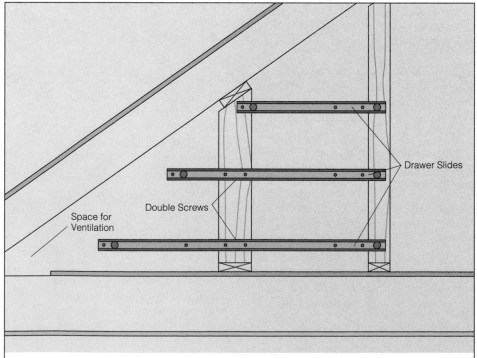

Drawer Slides

Double Screws

Space for Ventilation

4 Install side-mounted roller-bearing drawer slides on the drawers and wall studs.

UTILITY STORAGE

The areas of a home most used for storage are probably the basement and garage. No doubt they are also the most cluttered. Efficient use of space in these areas means getting things off the floor and organizing them.

Basement & Garage Storage

Two major concerns when considering basement or garage storage are moisture and temperature variations, respectively. Follow the guidelines given in previous chapters regarding the storage of items like fabric, clothing, and paper.

The basement and garage are traditionally the prime areas commandeered for use as a workshop. You can build a workbench to be the focal point of the workshop area and install perforated hardboard to hang tools and other equipment for fast utility storage. You can also build sturdy utility shelving in these areas.

In the garage, you have a large storage area you may never have thought of: the area just above the car. You can build a rack for holding all kinds of unwieldy building materials, such as extra molding and lumber, as well as sporting equipment like skis. The basement has some found space of its own. Build storage drawers into the space below the basement steps, and you have customized hideaway storage, even for a finished basement.

Basic Workbench

This workbench should take about 5 to 6 hours to build. The materials list is for a bench that's 72 inches long, 36 inches wide, and 36 inches high. Should you want one larger or smaller, you can adjust the materials to accommodate your own size bench. Use Douglas fir, if possible, for all the lumber.

Materials List

1	4x8-foot sheet of ¾-inch plywood (or particleboard)
3	12-foot 2x6s (for under plywood top)
2	12-foot 2x8s (for body)
1	10-foot 2x8 (for body)
1	12-foot 4x4 (for legs)
1	12-foot 2x4 (for bottom shelf)
3	12-foot 1x4s (for shelf planks)
3	4x4 shelf brackets
12	6½x½-inch carriage bolts with washers and nuts
2	1-pound boxes of 16d common nails
1	1-pound box of 8d common nails
1	1-pound box of 6d common nails

1 **Assembling the Body.** Cut the 12-foot 4x4 into four 36-inch sections to form the legs. Cut a 12-foot 2x8 into two 6-foot pieces to form the front and back boards. Now cut the remaining 2x8s into seven 33-inch boards. These pieces will be called joists. Cut the 12-foot 2x4 into two 69-inch lengths to form the shelf boards. Cut the 1x4s into 33-inch sections as the shelf planks. Lastly, cut the sheet of plywood into a 72 x 36-inch rectangle to serve as the bench top.

Lay the front and back boards side by side flat on the floor. Mark on 12-inch centers the spaces for the joists to be attached. Attach the joists to the front and back boards using four 16d nails on each side.

2 **Fastening the Legs.** With the frame on the floor, set each 4x4 leg into each corner, drilling two ⅝-inch holes through the front and back boards just barely into each leg. Also drill a ⅝-inch hole into each leg through the side joists. Make sure that the holes you drill in the side joists are between the two holes you drilled through the front and back boards. Remove each leg and finish drilling the holes. Put the legs back in place, then slip the carriage bolts, washers, and nuts into place and finger-tighten the legs to the frame.

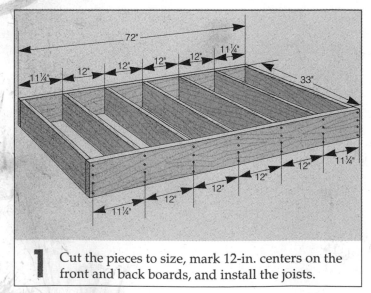

1 Cut the pieces to size, mark 12-in. centers on the front and back boards, and install the joists.

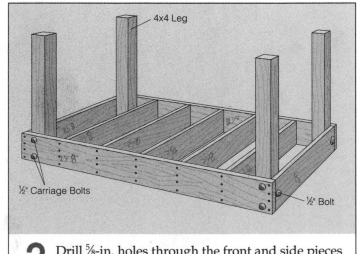

2 Drill ⅝-in. holes through the front and side pieces and the legs, then attach the carriage bolts.

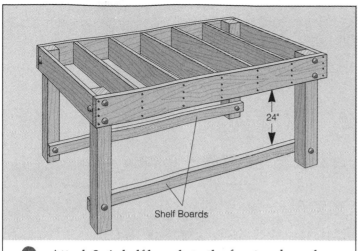

3 Attach 2x4 shelf boards to the front and rear legs 24 in. down from the face boards.

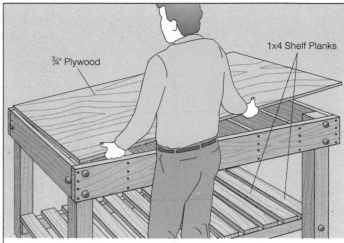

4 Install the plywood top and the 1x4 shelf planks with 1¼-in. drywall screws.

3 **Installing the Shelf Boards.** With all the legs in place, turn the bench upright. Measure down 24 inches from under the 2x8 front and back boards on each leg. From this point make a mark 1¾ inches down and 1¾ inches in from the edge of the 4x4, and drill holes through the 4x4s at this mark. Now measure in 1¾ inches from each end of the 2x4 shelf boards and make a mark in the middle of the board. Drill holes at these .marks and attach the boards to the legs with the carriage bolts, washers, and nuts. Now tighten all the nuts.

4 **Fastening the Top.** Put the plywood on top of the 2x8 joists, and fasten the plywood work surface to the joists. Use 1¼-inch drywall screws so you can easily remove the work surface. Lastly, lay the planks along the shelf boards like railroad ties and screw them to the shelf boards, also with 1¼-inch screws.

Perforated Hardboard Panels

Hand tools you often use, such as hammers, squares, pliers, screwdrivers, and others, can be hung in plain sight on a perforated hardboard panel. It's best to place the panel behind a workbench if you have one.

Installing the Panel

Wall studs are often exposed in unfinished spaces like basements and garages. If the studs are not exposed where you want to hang the perforated hardboard panel, locate them with a stud finder or by probing the wall with a thin nail or scratch awl. Cut three 1x3 or similar furring strips to the height of the perforated hardboard panel, and fasten them to the wall studs. Use 2½-inch drywall screws instead of nails in case you want to move the panel in the future. Lastly, screw the perforated hardboard panel to the furring strips with the same 2½-inch drywall screws. Use perfo-

rated-board hangers to hang equipment on the board. You can buy the hangers in home center and hardware stores.

Utility Shelving

Utility shelving is a quick and simple solution to storage problems. It requires only inexpensive materials and basic tools and techniques. You can fill a wall with shelves in one afternoon. Such shelving is best placed in the basement or utility room. A clever way to provide quick shelving is to use "L" shaped utility brackets.

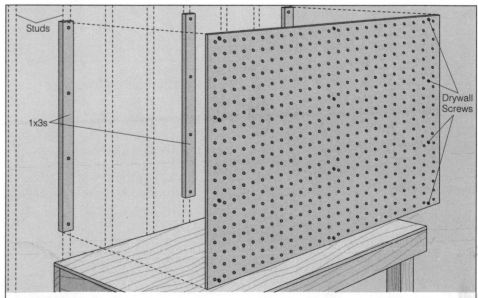

Installing the Panel. Fasten three 1x3 furring strips to the wall studs and hang the perforated hardboard panel with 2½-in. screws.

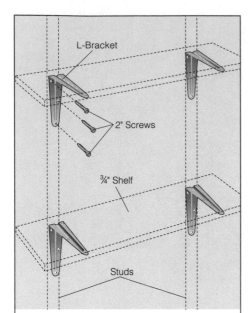

Installing Shelving with Brackets. Determine the height of your shelves, then screw the brackets to wall studs.

1 Measure up 15¼ in. from the floor and mark a 72-in.-long level line on the wall. Then mark four more lines, each 16 in. apart.

2 Attach five 1x2 cleats to the wall on the guidelines with 3½-in.-long drywall screws driven into studs.

Installing Shelving with Brackets

Decide where you would like to hang the shelves. With a stud finder, locate and mark studs within a suitable wall. Then, using a 48-inch level, mark the height of the proposed shelf less the thickness of the shelving material.

Using the stud lines and the horizontal lines across them, align the brackets and fasten them to the wall with 2-inch drywall screws. Make sure all the brackets align with one another by laying a level across them. Attach the shelving to the brackets from underneath with short (⅝-inch) wood screws.

Installing Built-in-Place Utility Shelving

Built-in-place shelves are great for the garage and basement, but don't overlook other parts of the house where clutter tends to accumulate and wall space is available. These shelves will also serve well in a pantry or utility shed. As a rule of thumb, support shelves at least every 36 inches, though that will vary depending on what you place on the shelving.

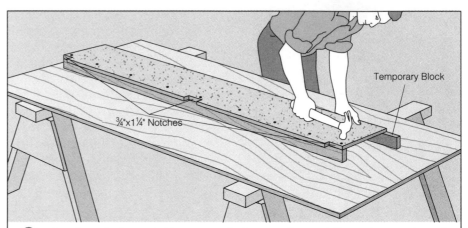

3 Cut five shelves 12x72 in., notch them in the middle and on each end, and nail 1x2 ribs on the front.

1 **Marking Level Lines.** Measure 15¼ inches up the wall from the floor and mark the first 72-inch-long level line. Then scribe four more, each 16 inches above the previous one.

2 **Installing the Cleats.** With a stud finder locate and mark each stud. Draw a plumb line where the studs intersect the horizontal lines. Cut 10 1x2 cleats to 72 inches long. Mark, drill, and install five cleats. Align the first cleat immediately beneath a level line, and attach it with one 3½-inch wood screw driven into the middle stud.

Mark where the other four studs cross the cleat, predrill pilot holes, and secure the cleat to the wall. Secure the remaining cleats.

3 **Notching the Shelves and Installing the Ribs.** Cut the five shelves from ¾-inch plywood to 12x72 inches. Use a saber saw to cut a 1½x¾-inch notch in the center of the front edge of each shelf. Cut same-size notches at each front corner. Use glue and 4d finishing nails to fasten the remaining cleats as front ribs flush with the back of the notches.

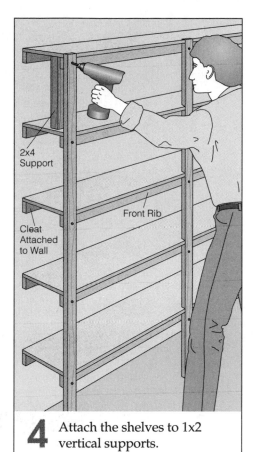

4 Attach the shelves to 1x2 vertical supports.

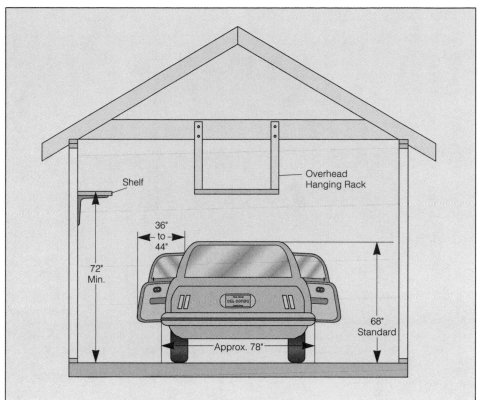

Garage Storage. Make use of space in the garage by installing ceiling racks, shelving in front of the car, or shelves on the walls above car-door height.

4 **Installing the Shelves.** Cut three 1x2 vertical supports to 80 inches, and cut a temporary brace from a scrap 2x4 to 15¼ inches. Lay a shelf on the bottom cleat, and prop it by placing the brace behind the rib at the center notch. Check that the shelf is level from front to back. Put the center vertical support in place, and screw it to the rib with a 1¼-inch drywall screw. Move the prop to behind one side notch, and make sure the shelf is level along its length and from front to back. Attach a side vertical support. Repeat for the other side. Then repeat the process for all the shelves, supporting the brace on the shelf below.

Garage Storage

It's difficult to find adequate space for shelving around a vehicle. An average single-car garage is almost 22 feet long and about 12 feet wide. The maximum dimensions for standard automobiles are 18 feet 5 inches in length, 78 inches in width, and 68

inches in height (standard vans: about 80 inches). And when a car door is opened, it juts out to a distance of 36 inches to 44 inches. There are areas in the garage where you may be able to create additional storage space, however, such as in front of the car, directly above the car, and to the sides of the car at a height clearing typical headroom.

If you add storage to the back of a garage, put in a wheel bumper that will prevent an automobile from moving too far into the garage and damaging stored items and shelving. Drive the car into the garage, then position a concrete parking bumper so that the car does not hit anything. You can buy concrete bumpers like the ones found in parking lots at a masonry supplier. You can also use an 8x8 timber as a bumper. Of course, when a different car is driven into the garage, check to see whether its clearances are similar.

Shelves placed to the side of an automobile should be at a height of at least 84 inches to provide

sufficient clearance for people to pass underneath. Avoid putting shelving directly to the side of the automobile's doors. Too much clutter here can make maneuvering in the garage difficult. There should be approximately 36 inches from the side of the car to the nearest obstacle or wall. This spacing ensures comfortable maneuvering.

Installing a Hanging Rack

Usually there are several feet above a typical car's roof that can be used for storage. A pair of brackets to form a rack can hold long, narrow items like fishing poles, spare tubing, piping, or light lumber and moldings. You can build such an overhead rack using typical perpendicular firewood stand brackets and some short sections of 2x4 lumber.

1 **Hanging the Legs.** One at a time, fasten four 2x4 legs to the ceiling joists of the garage with ½x3½-inch carriage bolts. Space the legs about 2 to 3 feet apart and

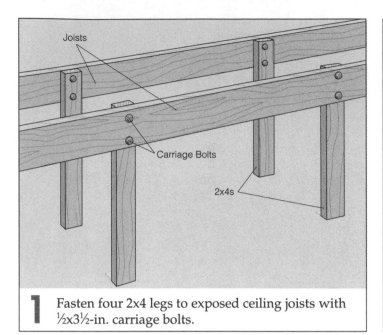

1 Fasten four 2x4 legs to exposed ceiling joists with ½x3½-in. carriage bolts.

Joists

Carriage Bolts

2x4s

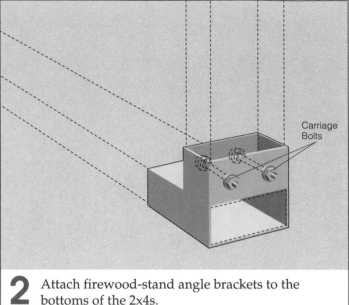

2 Attach firewood-stand angle brackets to the bottoms of the 2x4s.

Carriage Bolts

cut them long enough to hang at a suitable height, depending on the garage ceiling height.

2 Installing the Hardware.
Attach perpendicular angle brackets to the bottom of each leg. Drill holes through the 2x4s using the predrilled bracket holes as a template. Slip ½x2-inch carriage bolts through the bracket and 2x4. Insert 14½-inch 2x4 bottom rails through the brackets and secure them to the brackets with wood screws.

Note: Make sure before you start that there is ample clearance of the garage door when it is open. Also, check clearances for other cars that may be driven into the garage.

Under-Stair Drawers

Ordinarily, the staircase leading to the basement has considerable dead space underneath it. This space is also difficult to gain access to because getting at something in the low end involves removing everything in front. You can solve this storage predicament by building a bank of drawers under the staircase. With sliding drawers, you have easy access to everything stored under the stairs.

Building the Drawer Bank

1 Fastening the Framing Plates.
Stairs are infamous for collecting dust. Dust easily penetrates between treads and risers and gets deposited under the staircase. First, nail or screw a sheet of ¼-inch lauan plywood to the underside of the carriage, and seal the edges with common latex caulking. This should protect the contents of the drawers from dust falling from the stairs.

Recess the front wall plates back ¾ inch behind the finished face of the unit. Fasten corresponding rear plates against the rear wall under the staircase. Make certain that the front and rear plates are exactly parallel with one another. If you're attaching the plates to a masonry floor or wall, use spots of mastic adhesive and an occasional masonry nail or anchor. Make sure the bottom plate is level, and shim it if necessary.

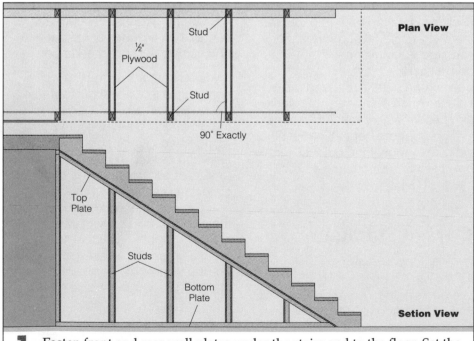

Stud

½" Plywood

Stud

Plan View

90° Exactly

Top Plate

Studs

Bottom Plate

Setion View

1 Fasten front and rear wall plates under the stairs and to the floor. Set the front wall back ¾ in.

2 **Installing the Studs.** Using a level, fasten the studs plumb and perpendicular to the bottom plates. Use only straight and square lumber; 2x3 or 2x4 dimensional lumber will suit. The distance between studs is up to your discretion and will represent the approximate width of your drawers. Don't exceed a drawer width of 36 inches.

The rear wall studs must also be perpendicular and in alignment with the front wall studs. Check to see that the distance between both front and rear studs is the same.

3 **Sheathing the Studs.** Cover the studs with ½-inch shop-grade plywood, spanning from front to rear. The sheathing will form the interior partitions between the drawer banks and provide a substrate to which you can fasten your drawer hardware.

4 **Attaching the Drawer Hardware.** After deciding the size and quantity of your drawers, lay out where you'll position them. Buy enough bottom side-mounted drawer slides for the number of drawers you want to install. When you install them, be sure that the

fronts of the slides are flush with the face of the framing. Fasten the cabinet-mounted side of the slides to the plywood where the bottom of each drawer will be. Manufacturers' installation instructions may vary, so follow the directions carefully.

5 **Building the Drawers.** You'll build these drawers the same way those in the window seat are built (page 55). Use ¾-inch plywood for the sides, back, and front, and hardwood plywood for the false front panel. Use ⅜-inch plywood for the bottom.

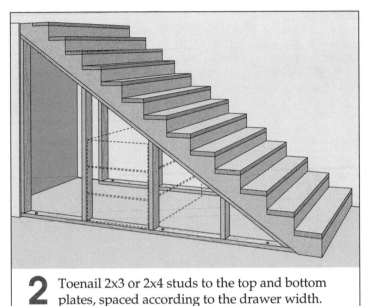

2 Toenail 2x3 or 2x4 studs to the top and bottom plates, spaced according to the drawer width.

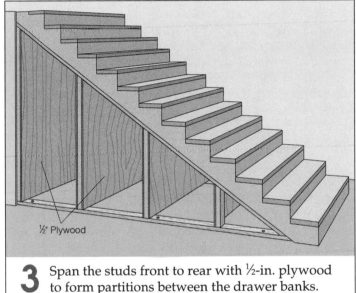

½" Plywood

3 Span the studs front to rear with ½-in. plywood to form partitions between the drawer banks.

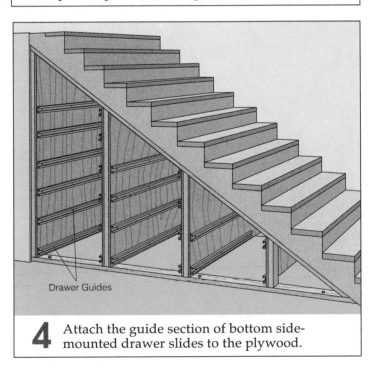

Drawer Guides

4 Attach the guide section of bottom side-mounted drawer slides to the plywood.

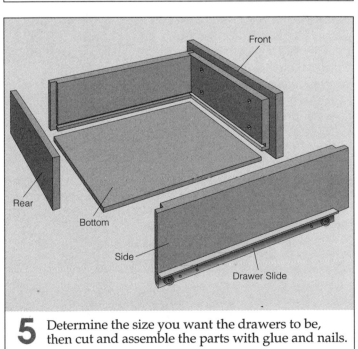

Front

Rear

Bottom

Side

Drawer Slide

5 Determine the size you want the drawers to be, then cut and assemble the parts with glue and nails.

Determine how deep you want the drawers to be and cut the sides and front accordingly. You'll lose ⅝ inch because of the bottom (⅜ inch for the depth of the panel and ¼ inch of clearance below the bottom panel), so take this dimension into account when you figure the drawer depth. Measure the distance from the face front wall to the rear, and cut the sides to size. Cut the rear panel to the proper depth. The rear panel rests on top of the bottom panel, so take this into account when you measure. Cut ¼x¾-inch rabbets in the front and back of the two side pieces to accept the front and back panels. Cut the front, back, and bottom panels to match the distance between the studs, less 1½ inches (allowing for ½ inch of clearance on each side of the drawer for the slide hardware). Cut the bottom to the same length as the sides, less ½ inch. Cut ¼x⅜-inch grooves for the bottom panel in the side and front pieces, ¼ inch up from the bottom edges.

Assemble the front and two sides with glue and 3d finishing nails. Slide the bottom panel into place, then attach the back panel with glue and 3d nails. Attach the bottom panel to the rear with ¾-inch brads. Cut the false front to size, but don't attach it yet.

Using the small screws that accompany your drawer hardware, fasten the slides to the bottom sides of the drawers, flush with the front. Once you've installed the hardware, slide the drawers into place. Using a straightedge, check to see that the drawers, when closed, are flush with the outside face of the framing. If any of the drawers are not flush, adjust the hardware until they are.

6 Installing the Face Sections. To keep the grain of the drawer fronts, angled sections, and toe kick in the same direction, you may wish to cut them from the same sheet of hardwood plywood. Finish each of the cut edges with veneer tape.

Each drawer bank has a triangular unfinished section at the top where you can't put a drawer. You'll have to install angled face sections in these areas. Figure the required angles with a level and protractor, or with a sliding bevel, and cut a template for each section out of cardboard. Make sure the left edge of each section overlays the framing by 1⅛ inches. Cut these sections from the same stock you'll use for the drawer fronts. Attach the sections to the stud framing with adhesive and 3d finishing nails.

Along the bottom of the unit, place a 2-to 4-inch toe kick on the face side of the bottom plate. The toe kick should be cut from the same stock as the drawer fronts.

With the angled sections and toe kick as your guide, attach the drawer fronts to the drawers. Cut the drawer fronts so that they overlay the partition walls by 1⅛ inches. With this spacing, you'll have a ¼-inch space between drawers when the entire unit is closed, and you won't see any framing, giving the unit a true built-in look.

From the inside of the drawer, fasten the drawer fronts with wood screws. One screw in each corner will suffice. Avoid gluing the drawer fronts to the drawers; if you do, adjusting the drawer fronts later will be much more difficult. Try to keep a uniform spacing of ³⁄₁₆ to ¼ inch between the drawer fronts, angled sections, and toe kick.

Lastly, locate the center of each drawer bank and mark the vertical centers of each drawer. Then cross these vertical marks with centered horizontal marks on each drawer and install drawer pulls where the lines intersect.

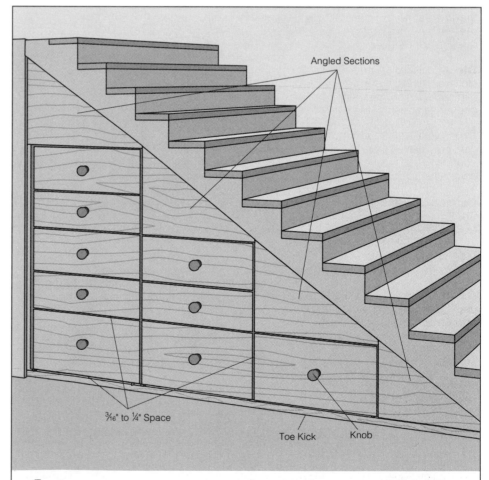

Angled Sections

³⁄₁₆" to ¼" Space

Toe Kick   Knob

6 Cut the face parts from a sheet of hardwood plywood and finish the edges with veneer tape. Make sure each drawer front and triangle section overlays the framing by 1⅛ in., for a ¼-in. space between drawers.

Air Barrier. An air-infiltration barrier or house wrap that can be used to protect a storage area in the attic from moisture and dust.

Back Clip. A plastic-coated metal hook-like clip attached to the wall, used for securing coated-wire systems to closet walls.

Carcase. A cabinet or chest frame.

Cedar Linings. Tongue-and-groove paneling made from cedar wood and installed behind clothes rods and shelving to protect clothing from damage by moth larvae.

Center Panels. The vertical panels that make up the center partition of a laminated-particleboard storage unit, with holes drilled on both sides to hold adjustable shelving brackets.

Circular Shelves. Rotating shelves that make it easy to reach items in the rear section of a corner cabinet; also referred to as a Lazy Susan.

Clothes Rod. A pole for hanging clothes in a wardrobe closet, usually with minimum linear dimensions of 5 feet for one person and 10 feet for two.

Coated-Wire System. A prefabricated closet organizing system whose components (shelves, baskets, etc.) consist of plastic-coated wire.

Custom-Built Storage Systems. Shelving and storage systems that are built to order.

Dado. A kind of groove that runs across the grain.

Dead Space. Wasted space in closets, under staircases, in corners, and under furniture that is suitable for storage.

Drawer Slide. A guide on which a drawer slides when it is opened.

End Panels. The vertical panels that serve as the end sides of a laminated-particleboard storage unit, with holes drilled on the left or right sides to hold adjustable shelving brackets.

Face Frame. A frame of stiles and rails that is applied to the face of a cabinet for style and strength. The face frame is often used to hide plywood edges.

Folding Attic Stairways. Ladder-like stairs easily pulled down to provide access to an attic.

Groove. A channel cut into a piece of wood that runs with the grain.

Joiner Plates. Plastic plates attached to the lip of coated-wire shelving to which support braces are attached.

Kneewall. A wall built from the attic floor to the angled roof rafters above. Drawer units can be installed between the studs of kneewalls.

Laminated Particleboard. Panels of particleboard that are laminated with a plastic surface material and are used in making storage systems.

Overdoor Hook. Hanging units, such as hooks and baskets, that are attached to the back of a door with metal clips. The clips are thin enough to fit in the clearance space between the door and the jamb.

Particleboard. A term used to describe several different kinds of sheet material made from ground-up bits of wood and adhesive.

Perforated Hardboard. Panel material, usually ¼ inch thick, manufactured from pressed wood fiber and perforated with a series of holes. Perforated hardboard is often used as wall material in workshops and garages where it serves as a place to hang tools; also known as pegboard or perf-board.

Piano Hinge. A long butt hinge used in making a chest or other piece of cabinetry.

Plywood. Veneers of wood glued together in a sandwich. Each veneer is oriented perpendicularly to the next.

PVC Laundry Basket. A frame constructed from polyvinyl chloride (PVC) pipes that is designed to hold a drawstring mesh laundry bag.

Rabbet. A ledge cut along one edge of a workpiece.

Reach-in Closet. The conventional bedroom clothes closet, measuring at least 24 inches deep and, for each person using it, a minimum of 60 inches wide.

Roll-Out Tray Dividers. A vertical storage unit with a roll-out rack designed for a kitchen base cabinet to hold large shallow pans, cutting boards, cookie sheets, and the like.

Soft-Netting Corner Shelves. A tightly bound fisherman's net hung across the corner of a child's bedroom used to hold stuffed animals and other lightweight toys.

Standard-and-Shelf Systems. Metal pieces ranging in length from 12 to 144 inches that are surface-mounted to walls with screws to hold shelves. Shelf brackets fit into slots located about every ½ to 1 inch so shelves can be adjusted.

Stemware Hanger. A storage rack for hanging stemware upside down that is placed under a cabinet to save room inside the cabinets.

Storage Chest-Seat. A chest that functions both as a seat and a storage place for bed linens.

Support Brackets. Metal L-shaped support fixtures that are used to fasten shelves to wall studs.

Tempered Hardboard. Solid or perforated hardboard panels impregnated with resin under high pressure to make them stronger and more resistant to moisture.

Tiered Frame. A coated-wire framing system in which baskets are placed on separate levels.

Tilt-Out Tray. The storage space created behind a sink base's false front panel used for hiding soap, sponges, steel-wool pads, and other cleaning accessories.

Uprights. The vertical members of a shelving or storage system.

Utility Storage. Areas in the garage and basement of a house used for storing items such as tools and sporting equipment.

Walk-in Closet. A closet measuring a minimum of 84 inches wide by 72 inches deep.

INDEX